THE IDIOT

Borgo Press Books Translated by FRANK J. MORLOCK

FYODOR DOSTOYEVSKY'S THE IDIOT

A PLAY IN THREE ACTS

by

FRANK J. MORLOCK

From the Novel by Fyodor Dostoyevsky

————————

THE BORGO PRESS

An Imprint of Wildside Press LLC

MMIX

Copyright © 2009 by Frank J. Morlock

www.wildsidebooks.com

FIRST WILDSIDE EDITION

CONTENTS

DEDICATION

TO THE MEMORY OF MY FATHER AND MOTHER

ABOUT FRANK J. MORLOCK

FRANK J. MORLOCK has written and translated many plays since retiring from the legal profession in 1992. His translations have also appeared on Project Gutenberg, the Alexandre Dumas Père web page, Literature in the Age of Napoléon, Infinite Artistries.com, and Munsey's (formerly Blackmask). In 2006 he received an award from the North American Jules Verne Society for his translations of Verne's plays. He lives and works in México.

CAST OF CHARACTERS

The Epanchin Doorman
Myshkin
Ganya
General Epanchin
Madame Epanchin
Aglaia Epanchin
Ferdyshtchenko
General Ivolgin
Nina Ivolgin
Varya Ivolgin
Nastasya Fillipovna
Rogozhin
Lebedyev
Rogozhin's Roughnecks
Totsky
Nastasya's Footman
Katya
Antip Burdovsky
Ippolit Terentyev
Vladimir Lebedyev

ACT I

Scene 1

General Epanchin's home. The main stage represents the parlor of a Russian house in the 1880s. In the center rear is an anteroom leading to the entrance.

DOORMAN
Step into the parlor and leave your bundle here.

MYSHKIN
If you'll allow me, I'd rather wait with you: what am I to do in there alone?

DOORMAN
You can't stay here. You are a visitor. Visitors are guests. Guests must wait in the parlor. Therefore you must wait in the parlor.

(puzzled) You really want to see General Epanchin himself?

MYSHKIN
Yes, I have business.

DOORMAN
That's no concern of mine. My business is only to announce you but I've told you already I won't unless the secretary allows it.

(hesitates) Are you really from abroad?

MYSHKIN
You mean, am I really Prince Myshkin? Yes, to both questions.

DOORMAN
Are you a mind reader?

MYSHKIN
I assure you I haven't told a lie. It's just that I am not in very flourishing circumstances right now.

DOORMAN
I have no doubt on that score. You are asking General Epanchin for assistance?

MYSHKIN
Oh, no.

DOORMAN
You must excuse me. The General is busy just now.

MYSHKIN
Then if you don't mind, if I have to wait a long while, is there anywhere I could smoke?

DOORMAN
Smoke? Of course not: you should be ashamed of yourself.

MYSHKIN
Oh, I didn't mean in this room. But I haven't smoked in three hours and I'm used to it.

DOORMAN
Now how am I to announce a, a—person—like you. You won't go in the parlor. A guest who won't go in the par-

lor? Unheard of! You are not thinking of staying with the family?

MYSHKIN
Oh, no. I just dropped in to make their acquaintance.

DOORMAN
What? You just said you had business!

MYSHKIN
Well you see Madame Epanchin is a Princess Myshkin. And the last of them. There are no Myshkins left but she and I.

DOORMAN
(Aghast) Then you are a relation.

MYSHKIN
Very distant. I wrote Madame Epanchin from abroad but she didn't answer me. Nonetheless, I thought I should look her up.

DOORMAN
You really ought to go into the parlor.

MYSHKIN
But then how should I have explained it to you? Now, perhaps, you could announce me without waiting for the secretary.

DOORMAN
I can't. His Excellency gave special orders not to be disturbed this morning. Only Ganya Ivolgin goes in without being announced.

MYSHKIN
Who is he?

DOORMAN
He is the secretary.

MYSHKIN
And Madame Epanchin, when does she see visitors?

DOORMAN
Whenever she takes it in her head.

MYSHKIN
Tell me, is my Russian acceptable? I've been away a long time and I haven't spoken more than a half dozen words of Russian for the last two years.

DOORMAN
Why, your Russian is excellent, Prince—it's the things you say that are unusual. Have you been away long?

MYSHKIN
Many years.

(Pause) On the train people were talking about the New Courts of Justice. What are they?

DOORMAN
They are modeled on European courts. Are the European courts really better?

MYSHKIN
I don't think so. We have no capital punishment here.

DOORMAN
Do they in Europe?

MYSHKIN
Yes, I'm afraid they do. I saw a man guillotined in France.

DOORMAN
Did he scream?

MYSHKIN
There is no time. Ah, that man was weeping.

(Excited) It is written "thou shalt no kill", so because he has killed are we to kill him? It's an outrage!

DOORMAN
At least there is not much pain.

MYSHKIN
Everyone says that. But what if the worst pain is not the bodily suffering but the certainty of annihilation? Ah, legal murder is worse than ordinary murder because it takes away a man's last hope. No! You can't treat a man like that!

DOORMAN
(Friendly now) If you really want to smoke—it's against the rules, but—

(Ganya enters from the direction of the study)

DOORMAN
This gentleman, sir—announces himself as Prince Myshkin.

GANYA
You are the Prince Myshkin who sent a letter to Madame Epanchin about a year ago?

MYSHKIN
Yes.

GANYA
And you are not here to borrow money?

(Myshkin shakes his head) Then I'm sure they will receive you.

(He returns to the study) I'll tell the General.

(General Epanchin returns with Ganya)

EPANCHIN
Prince Myshkin? What can I do for you?

MYSHKIN
I have just returned from Switzerland, where I have stayed four years because of my health. My hope is simply to make your acquaintance.

EPANCHIN
I have little time for making acquaintances but as you no doubt have some object...

MYSHKIN
I knew you would think that but the only reason for my visit is the pleasure of meeting you.

EPANCHIN
It is, of course, a pleasure for me, too, but—

MYSHKIN
We have little in common, of course. But I return to Russia knowing no one. I must begin to make friends. And as you are the only person known to me I thought I would begin with you. We might, perhaps, be of use to one another.

(Musing)— I had heard that you were good people—

EPANCHIN
Much obliged. Where are you staying?

MYSHKIN

I haven't found a place yet.

EPANCHIN

(Worried) So you've come straight here? And with luggage?

MYSHKIN

My luggage is a little bundle of linen. I shall have time to take a room this evening.

EPANCHIN

(Relieved) For a moment I thought you planned to stay here.

MYSHKIN

(Smiling) Only on your invitation. But actually not even then; not for any reason, but simply because that's the way I am.

EPANCHIN

(Blunt) Just as well that I haven't invited you and don't intend to. I might as well make things clear—there is no question of family between us—so there is nothing but—

MYSHKIN

(Amused) Nothing but to get up and go? I knew it would be this way. Well goodbye and forgive me for troubling you.

EPANCHIN

(A little bit ashamed) Don't go yet, Prince. I'm sure my wife would like to meet you—if you have time—

MYSHKIN

Oh, I have time. I'm really here only to make friends, not for assistance. But I don't want to be in the way.

EPANCHIN
Well if you're as you seem to be I shall be very happy to make your acquaintance. How old are you?

MYSHKIN
Twenty-six.

EPANCHIN
I took you to be younger. Tell me, have you any means at all or do you intend to take up some kind of work?

MYSHKIN
I hadn't more than my return fare upon returning. I have no money at all.

EPANCHIN
How do you intend to live?

MYSHKIN
I hope to get some kind of work.

EPANCHIN
But are you trained to any profession?

MYSHKIN
No—you see I was very ill. Epilepsy. A Mr. Pavlishtchev used to pay my expenses in Switzerland but he died suddenly two years ago.

EPANCHIN
Pavlishtchev. Why, I knew him myself. Why did he pay your expenses?

MYSHKIN
That's something I've never been able to quite understand. But he did, until his death....

EPANCHIN
And you have no one? Absolutely no one?

MYSHKIN
At the moment on one. I have, however, received a letter....

EPANCHIN
Have you at least trained for something that your affliction would not prevent you from undertaking? Some easy post, for instance?

MYSHKIN
Oh, my illness would not prevent me. But I don't really know what I am fit for.

EPANCHIN
Can you write Russian without mistakes?

MYSHKIN
Oh, yes, and my writing is excellent. I am quite a calligraphist. Let me give you a specimen.

EPANCHIN
By all means. And I like your readiness, Prince. You are very nice, I must say. Ganya, give the Prince some writing materials.

(Ganya does so, and Prince Myshkin busies himself)

(Ganya shows the General a portrait)

GANYA
See! It came today. At last!

EPANCHIN
Nastasya Fillipovna! Did she send it to you herself?

GANYA
From her own hand.

EPANCHIN
She promised Count Totsky and myself that tonight, at her party, she would give you her final word. To be or not to be.

GANYA
Did she say that positively?

EPANCHIN
Yes, but she said not to tell you beforehand.

GANYA
Remember that she has left me free until she makes up her mind.

EPANCHIN
You're not going to back out now?

GANYA
I didn't say that....

EPANCHIN
Are you having trouble at home?

GANYA
What difference does it make? Father is playing the fool as usual. Mother does nothing but cry; my sister hardly speaks to me. But I am my own master. If I choose to marry a whore I—

EPANCHIN
You're all taking this very strangely. Nastasya hasn't lived with Totsky for years now. And this is your big opportunity. The Count has promised seventy-five thousand rubles to you.

MYSHKIN
(Looking up) So that's Nastasya Fillipovna. How beautiful!

EPANCHIN
But surely you don't know her.

MYSHKIN
No, but I know of her.

GANYA
How is this?

MYSHKIN
On the train I met a man named—named Rogozhin who was returning from Germany to claim his inheritance. He was in love with her before he left. It seems he got in trouble because of her. He misappropriated money of his father's to buy her a gift and his father sent him to Germany. Now his father is dead.

GANYA
Ah, the affair of the earrings. I have heard it before, too. But now it's a different matter. His father was enormously wealthy. I only hope nothing sensational will come of it.

MYSHKIN
Are you afraid of his millions? You are not, of course.

EPANCHIN
Is he a fool or a serious person, Prince?

MYSHKIN
He said he was coming back to claim her. I don't know. I fancied he was capable of almost any excess.

EPANCHIN
Then it will all depend on how it strikes her.

GANYA
(Laughing) And you know what she is like sometimes.

EPANCHIN
Then don't, whatever you do, contradict her too much to-day. Why are you grinning? You know there is no question of my gaining anything in this.

GANYA
(Flat voice) No. You won't.

EPANCHIN
Then why do you seem so pleased that this Rogozhin has turned up? Are you going to marry her?

GANYA
(Morosely) I am.

EPANCHIN
Well that settles that. Now, Prince, let's have a look.

(Looking) Aha. That's prize copy. Splendid!

GANYA
(Impressed) He IS an artist. You have a vocation.

EPANCHIN
There's a career in it. I think I can get you a job. I've decided to lend you some money.

(Puts up his hand) You can repay me whenever it's convenient. Next we must find a place for you to stay. Ganya's family takes lodgers. The terms are extremely moderate. And your salary will soon be sufficient to meet it. Is it agreeable to you, Ganya?

GANYA
Perfectly. Mother will be delighted.

MYSHKIN
You have been very kind to me....

EPANCHIN
I have a motive. You will learn it later. You see I am perfectly straightforward.

MYSHKIN
Since you are so kind—I have this letter that, perhaps....

(He starts to take it out)

EPANCHIN
Excuse me: I haven't a minute more now. I will inform my wife. Ganya get on with the accounts. Time. Time.

(Epanchin goes out, turning towards his wife's apartments)

GANYA
So you admire a woman like that, Prince?

MYSHKIN
Such an extraordinary face. She has obviously suffered. So proud. But I wonder if she is kind-hearted? That would redeem all.

GANYA
And would *you* marry such a woman?

MYSHKIN
I am an epileptic. I....

GANYA
And would Rogozhin marry her?

MYSHKIN
Yes. Tomorrow, and murder her in a week.

(Pause) Why, what's the matter?

GANYA
Oh, nothing. I must attend to the accounts. Excuse me, Prince.

(He goes into the study)

(General Epanchin, Madame Epanchin, and their daughter Aglaia enter)

EPANCHIN
Let me introduce Prince Myshkin, your namesake and your kinsman. My wife, your cousin—and my daughter, Aglaia. Make him welcome and be kind to him. But now you must all excuse me, I have an appointment.

MADAME EPANCHIN
(Irritated) We all know where you are hurrying off to.

EPANCHIN
Give him your albums, Mesdames. Let him write something for you. His handwriting is really exquisite.

MADAME EPANCHIN
Where are you off to?

EPANCHIN
I am going to the Count's. I'm late already. Good-bye for the present, Prince.

(He darts out)

MADAME EPANCHIN
He's going to see her.

AGLAIA
(Upset) Maman, we have company. How can you?

MADAME EPANCHIN
Don't interfere with me Aglaia! I'm sorry to be so rude, Prince, but— Anyway, sit here by me. I noticed you are not nearly so queer a creature as you were described to be. Perhaps the table napkin is not necessary. Did you have a napkin tied around your neck at mealtimes, Prince?

MYSHKIN
Not since I was seven.

AGLAIA
Mother, how can you mortify me so?

MADAME EPANCHIN
Quite right. And your fits?

MYSHKIN
Fits? My fits don't happen very often now. In fact, I haven't had one in two years.

AGLAIA
Mother!

MADAME EPANCHIN
It is not polite to whisper in company child.

(Musing) He speaks very well.

(In exasperation) So it was all stuff and nonsense as usual.

(Pause. She smiles, relieved) Come, Prince, tell me your story.

AGLAIA
(Really angry) I would never say anything if I were told to like that.

MADAME EPANCHIN
Why not? He has a tongue and I want to know. Tell me your first impression of Switzerland.

MYSHKIN
It was a strong impression...

MADAME EPANCHIN
There you see—

AGLAIA
Do let him speak, at least, Maman.

(Whisper) This Prince is a great rogue and no idiot at all.

MYSHKIN
My first impression was a very strong one. The morning after I arrived in Basel I woke up in this beautiful strange country to the bray of an ass.

AGLAIA
(Laughs helplessly) An ass?

MADAME EPANCHIN
That's odd. Yet there's nothing funny about it. One may even fall in love with an ass.

AGLAIA
It happens all the time, mother.

MADAME EPANCHIN
She is a silly girl—go on, Prince.

MYSHKIN
I've been awfully fond of asses ever since. I began to learn about how useful a beast it is.

MADAME EPANCHIN
Why, what's so funny, Aglaia?

AGLAIA
I've seen an ass, Maman, and even heard one. That's all.

MADAME EPANCHIN
You must excuse her, Prince, she's kind but thoughtless.

MYSHKIN
I should have said the same thing. But still I defend the ass; the ass is a good natured and useful creature.

MADAME EPANCHIN
And are you good-natured, Prince?

AGLAIA
You must excuse her, Prince, she's kind but thoughtless.

MADAME EPANCHIN
(Aghast) Please believe me, Prince, I spoke thought-lessly—I—

MYSHKIN
(Laughing) Oh, I believe you.

MADAME EPANCHIN
I see you are a very good, kind, young man.

MYSHKIN
Not always.

MADAME EPANCHIN
Well, I am. It's a failing I have, even when I'm angry. Tell us about the things you learned in Switzerland.

MYSHKIN
Learned? Oh, I didn't learn much. But I was very happy

there.

AGLAIA
(Interestedly) Happy? You know how to be happy? Is it possible?

MYSHKIN
It's just that every minute was precious to me. It would be hard to say why. Before I went there I always dreamed of what I would do—in the future. There, I came to value the present so much that I could almost believe that a wealth of life was possible even between the four walls of a prison.

AGLAIA
That last edifying remark I read when I was twelve—in my reader.

MADAME EPANCHIN
The Prince is a philosopher.

AGLAIA
(Scornfully) Yes. The philosophy of living as cheaply as possible. How to get the most out of nothing.

MYSHKIN
This talk of prison reminds me of a story. In France I met a man who had been sentenced to death but was reprieved minutes before the execution was to take place. He had already been blindfolded. He was certain that he would die. But then he wondered: What if he were not to die? He thought he would grasp each moment of life and not waste one. The thought so depressed him that he longed to be shot immediately.

AGLAIA
Is that all?

MYSHKIN
Yes.

AGLAIA
But what did you tell that story for? What does it mean?

MYSHKIN
Oh, I was reminded of it by our conversation.

MADAME EPANCHIN
Did your friend live life better after his reprieve?

MYSHKIN
Oh, no. He nearly died of boredom.

AGLAIA
It's impossible to grasp each moment.

MYSHKIN
Yes. I know that. But I can't believe it.

AGLAIA
You think you will live more wisely than anyone?

MYSHKIN
Yes, I have thought that, too.

AGLAIA
And you think so still?

MYSHKIN
Yes. I think so still.

AGLAIA
That's modest.

MYSHKIN
Are you angry with me for preaching to you? I have lived

less than others you know.

AGLAIA
(Miffed) If you're happy, then you must have lived more, not less, than others. Why do you make a pretence and apologize? And you draw edifying reflections from everything. Life is easy like that.

MADAME EPANCHIN
I can't make out why you are so cross Aglaia.

AGLAIA
(To Madame Epanchin) It's all right, Maman.

(To Myshkin) But it's a pity you haven't seen an execution. I should like to ask you one question if you had.

MYSHKIN
I have witnessed one.

AGLAIA
Oh? I ought to have guessed it. That's the last straw! Well, did you like it? Was there much that was edifying and instructive?

MADAME EPANCHIN
Tell us about it.

MYSHKIN
I just described it a little while ago. It always upsets me to tell of it.

AGLAIA
Described it? To whom?

MYSHKIN
To your doorman.

MADAME EPANCHIN
That's odd.

AGLAIA
The Prince is a democrat. As soon as you tell us anything you seem to be ashamed of it. Why is that?

MADAME EPANCHIN
That's not clever, Aglaia. She's a tease but not a bad girl. She likes you. I know. I know her face.

MYSHKIN
I know her face, too.

AGLAIA
What do you mean?

MYSHKIN
I'll tell you afterwards.

AGLAIA
What solemnity! You are just trying to arouse our curiosity. And if you're such a connoisseur of faces you certainly must have been in love. Tell us about it.

MYSHKIN
I have never been in love. I have been happy in a different way.

AGLAIA
How? In what way?

MYSHKIN
All right, I'll tell you. It was in Switzerland. At the sanatorium there was a girl. I only kissed her once. She lived in our village. She was a scrub girl. A Frenchman had seduced and abandoned her. Her mother was always telling her what a disgrace she had brought on the family. The

children threw stones at her. Marie put up with everything because she believed it more than anyone. When her mother died the preacher preached a sermon against Marie. He blamed her for her mother's death.

I wanted to do something for her. So I pawned my watch and gave her the money. Then I kissed her, not for love but because I pitied her. Then I talked to the children who threw stones at her. I told them her whole story. Soon they were sorry for her and stopped throwing stones. It was funny; the children came over to my side but the town remained against her. The children threw stones at the preacher after that terrible sermon. It was the children that made her forget her unhappiness. She died of consumption. But she was happy. It was only after I left that I realized how much I loved children. It was then that I recalled their faces, their sweet faces. And that is how I understand faces. You, Madame Epanchin, are a perfect child in everything. In good and bad alike. You are not angry with me for saying so?

MADAME EPANCHIN
No. It is perfectly true. I knew about it before you told me. But why do you say nothing about Aglaia, Prince? She is waiting and so am I.

MYSHKIN
Your daughter is exceedingly beautiful.

MADAME EPANCHIN
So that's all. What of her qualities?

MYSHKIN
Beauty is a riddle.

AGLAIA
And are you good at riddles, Prince?

MADAME EPANCHIN
But she is beautiful, Prince.

MYSHKIN
Almost as beautiful as Nastasya Fillipovna.

AGLAIA
Oh, where did you see her?

MYSHKIN

Ganya had her portrait. I saw it.

MADAME EPANCHIN
Go get it from him, Prince!

MYSHKIN
If you like.

(He goes into the study)

MADAME EPANCHIN
He is nice, but much too simple. A little absurd, in fact.

AGLAIA
He managed to flatter us both!

MADAME EPANCHIN
Nonsense! He did not flatter me! He's like me. He's a child. But he's got his wits about him, exactly like me.

AGLAIA
Then he's not like you, Maman.

MYSHKIN
Here it is.

(He passes a note to Aglaia who gives him a look that says

she understands him)

MADAME EPANCHIN
Yes, good-looking.

AGLAIA
So that's the kind of beauty you appreciate, is it?

MYSHKIN
Yes.

AGLAIA
Why?

(She looks at the note absently, but then suddenly looks surprised)

MYSHKIN
In that face—there is much suffering.

AGLAIA
What power.

MADAME EPANCHIN
What are you talking about?

AGLAIA
Such beauty is power. With beauty like that one might turn the whole world upside down.

MADAME EPANCHIN
Stuff! Prince, will you call Ganya?

(Myshkin goes to the study)

AGLAIA
Maman!

MADAME EPANCHIN
I want a word with him. That's enough. We have nothing but secrets here.

AGLAIA
Maman, what are you saying?

MADAME EPANCHIN
What is it, dear daughter? As for the Prince's hearing it, we are friends.

(Myshkin returns with Ganya) So you are contemplating marriage?

GANYA
I beg your pardon?

MADAME EPANCHIN
Are you getting married?

GANYA
N-no—I n-no—

(He looks at Aglaia who looks coldly at him)

MADAME EPANCHIN
No. You said no. Enough. I shall remember that. Wednesday morning you have said no to my question. Good-bye. You have a lot to do, so here is your photograph. Give my regards to your unhappy mother. Good-bye, everyone.

(Madame Epanchin exits)

AGLAIA
Maman!

GANYA
Prince, I am just going home. If you've not changed your

plans about boarding with us I will take you.

AGLAIA
Stay a little, Prince. You must write in my album. I'll be back directly.

(She goes out, in the direction of the women's quarters)

GANYA
That was your doing. You're a shameless chatterbox.

MYSHKIN
I assure you that you are mistaken. I didn't even know you had intentions that way.

GANYA
You heard what I said to the General. You repeated it. You are lying. When else could they have heard it?

MYSHKIN
I haven't said a word about it.

GANYA
Did you give the note? Answer.

MYSHKIN
Yes.

(Aglaia returns)

AGLAIA
Here, Prince. Write me something.

(The Prince moves to the writing table)

GANYA

(To Aglaia) One word, one word from you and I am saved.

MYSHKIN
What am I to write?

AGLAIA
I will dictate to you. Ready? Write: "I don't make bargains". Then the day and the month.

(IIe does) Show it to me.

(He shows her) Excellent! You've written wonderfully. I want to give you something for a keepsake.

(She gives the note) Read this.

(Myshkin looks at her) I know you haven't read it, and this wretch cannot have confided in you. Read it. I want you to read it.

(He reads the note) I assure you it's all right. This man assures me that if I tell him to break off with Nastasya Fillipovna I am bound in no way to him. Notice how he underlines those words. And yet he knows that if he broke it himself without hoping for anything for me, I should have felt differently toward him. But he has a dirty soul. He knows it; but he can't bring himself to do it. Take the note and give it to him.

MYSHKIN
Am I to write an answer?

AGLAIA
Nothing, of course. That's the best answer. Be on your guard against him, Prince, he won't forgive you for returning his note—

(She laughs and goes out)

GANYA

So she won't make bargains. Then I will. I'll make her smart for it. But tell me this. What have you done to deserve to be treated as a confident? What did you say to them?

MYSHKIN

Certainly. I talked about Switzerland.

GANYA

Damn Switzerland!

MYSHKIN

Then we talked of capital punishment.

GANYA

Capital punishment.

MYSHKIN

Yes. Then I told them about a poor village girl.

GANYA

Damn the village girl. What else?

MYSHKIN

And that led me to commenting on their faces. And I said to Aglaia that she was almost as beautiful as Nastasya Fillipovna and that is how I came to mention the portrait.

GANYA

You didn't repeat what you heard earlier? You didn't? You didn't?

MYSHKIN

Positively.

GANYA

Then you missed something—oh, damned idiot!

MYSHKIN

I must tell you Ganya that once I was like an idiot. But then it was a long time ago. I can understand your anger but you've been abusive to me and so hadn't we better part?

GANYA

Excuse me, Prince. Forgive me. It's all a mess and I'm sure—but, of course, it's inexcusable. Prince, come as you intended.

MYSHKIN

Don't apologize, I understand how hard it is for you. I'll come with pleasure.

GANYA

Yes, and everything will be decided—Tonight.

CURTAIN

ACT I

Scene 2

The Ivolgins' living room, cheaply but pretentiously furnished.

GANYA
One word, Prince. Be so good if it won't be a bother to you—don't gossip here of what happened at the Epanchins. There's degradation enough. Restrain yourself, for today, anyway.

MYSHKIN
I assure you I gossiped much less than you think.

GANYA
What a horrid room. Well, that's not my business—I don't let the rooms.

(Exit Ganya, enter Ferdyshtchenko)

FERDYSHTCHENKO
I've come to warn you. Don't lend me any money for I shall certainly ask you.

MYSHKIN
Very well.

FERDYSHTCHENKO
Ferdyshtchenko. That's me. Do you mean to pay here?

MYSHKIN
Yes.

FERDYSHTCHENKO
Well, I don't. Tell me, can one exist with such a name as Ferdyshtchenko?

MYSHKIN
Why not?

FERDYSHTCHENKO
Good-bye.

(He goes out)

(Enter General Ivolgin, by another door)

IVOLGIN
It is he. It is he. The living picture. Prince Myshkin?

MYSHKIN
Yes.

IVOLGIN
General Ivolgin. I knew your father.

MYSHKIN
Is it possible? My father died twenty years ago.

IVOLGIN
We were in the service together.

MYSHKIN
Yes, he was in the Vassihkovsky regiment.

IVOLGIN
No, the Byelormirsky. He was transferred just before his death. I was at his bedside. Your mother...

MYSHKIN
Yes, she died six months later from a chill.

IVOLGIN
Not a chill. Not a chill. You can take my word for that, I was there. I was passionately in love with your mother. We almost quarreled over her, your father and I—in fact. You've come to live with us.

MYSHKIN
For a while.

IVOLGIN
I must warn you. Nina is my wife...and she is a rare woman. And my daughter, Varya—my daughter—but—but,—in fact, my son Ganya is about to contract a disgraceful marriage.

NINA
(Entering) Ah, Prince.

IVOLGIN
Only fancy that, my dear, it appears that I used to dandle the Prince in my arms. You remember Nikolay Ivanovitch? He was still at Tver when we were there.

NINA
I'm afraid I don't. Is that your father?

MYSHKIN
Yes. But it wasn't Tver but—

IVOLGIN
It was Tver. Your friend Pavlishtchev must have forgotten.

MYSHKIN
Did you know Pavlishtchev?

IVOLGIN
Yes, I blessed your father when he died.

NINA
Oh!

MYSHKIN
My father died when he was awaiting trial. I've never been able to discover what he was accused of.

IVOLGIN
Oh, that. Why he would have been acquitted.

MYSHKIN
What happened?

IVOLGIN
It was a strange affair. A Private Kolpakov had stolen some boot leather. The Prince caught him and gave him a dressing down and threatened to flog him. Very good. And what does this private do? He goes back to the barracks and dies. I ask you! Well then about six months later after we had buried this scoundrel he turns up again in another regiment of the same brigade.

MYSHKIN
Is it possible?

NINA
My husband—is mistaken.

IVOLGIN
Mistaken—nonsense. I was on the board of inquiry myself.

VARYA
(Who has been listening) Father, somebody wants you.

IVOLGIN
Yes, yes coming, coming....

(He goes out)

NINA
You must overlook my husband's "eccentricities". If my husband ever asks you for payment please tell him that you've paid me. It's just to keep from muddling accounts.

(To Varya) Varya, what's the matter?

VARYA
A present to him today from herself!

NINA
There's no hope left.

(Ganya enters)

GANYA
What? Ah, I understand. You're doing it again. Can't you be quiet?

NINA
I am not going to ask you anything you don't care to tell me of yourself I assure you. I am completely resigned. I shan't cry anymore. As for your sister....

GANYA
Ah, Varya again. Look I swear to you, again. No one will ever be lacking in respect for you—

NINA
Will it be settled tonight?

GANYA
Yes.

NINA

How can a woman so—so—?

GANYA

Experienced you mean?

NINA

(Bitterly) How can she send you her portrait when you don't love her? Can you have hoodwinked her so completely?

GANYA

There you go again. No reproaches and they've begun already. We'd better drop it. As for Varya, she can please herself about it. See how she glares at me—my sister.

VARYA

If she comes into this house I shall leave. I shall keep my word.

(The bell rings)

GANYA

Out of obstinacy! Don't snot at me! I don't give a damn!

(The bell rings, but the only one to hear it is Myshkin, who goes out and admits Nastasya Fillipovna)

GANYA

Well, the Prince has left us—good riddance. As for the rest of you....

NASTASYA

(In the hall) Are you going to announce me? What an idiot.

GANYA

You can all walk out.

MYSHKIN
Nastasya Fillipovna!

(Everything abruptly comes to a halt)

NASTASYA
What's the matter? Does no one answer the bell? Why do you look so upset, Ganya? Introduce me, please.

VARYA
In my case that won't be necessary.

GANYA
This is my mother, Nina Alexandrovna.

NINA
It is a pleasure....

NASTASYA
(Pays no attention) Where are the lodgers? You take lodgers don't you?

(Pause) Ganya?

GANYA
Why...?

NASTASYA
Wherever do you keep them? Does it pay? It's so small.

NINA
It's rather a bother, but....

NASTASYA
(Still paying no attention) How you look!

(To Ganya) My goodness, how you look this minute!

(She laughs)

MYSHKIN
(As Ganya starts to choke) Drink some water.

GANYA
Why, are you a doctor, Prince?

(Recovering) May I introduce you to Nastasya Fillipovna?

NASTASYA
Is he a Prince? Only fancy I took him for a footman, ha, ha, ha.

GANYA
Prince Myshkin.

NASTASYA
And I swear to you. I was ready to swear at you for a great booby, Prince. Forgive me, please. Tell me, why didn't you undeceive me just now?

MYSHKIN
I was a little taken aback.

NASTASYA
But how did you know my name? Although, I think I have seen you somewhere. And why were you taken aback? What is there so amazing about me?

MYSHKIN
I saw your portrait. And I feel as though I had seen you before somewhere, too.

NASTASYA
Where? Where?

MYSHKIN
Ah, but that is impossible. Perhaps in a dream.

(Ferdyshtchenko and the General enter)

FERDYSHTCHENKO
Bravo, Prince! You pay compliments well. And here is General Ivolgin, come to meet you, Nastasya.

IVOLGIN
General Ardalion Alexandrovitch Ivolgin. An old soldier. And the father of a family which is happy at the prospect of including such a charming—lady.

(Ferdyshtchenko gets him a seat) I've heard my son....

NASTASYA
You are a pretty one! Why do you never come and see me? Do you shut yourself up or is it your son's doing? It wouldn't compromise anyone....

IVOLGIN
Children of this century and their parents....

NINA
Nastasya Fillipovna, please excuse my husband for a moment, someone is asking to see him.

NASTASYA
Oh, but for a long time I've been waiting to see him. You won't leave me, General, you won't go away?

NINA
I promise you he shall come and see you but now he needs rest.

NASTASYA
Ardalion Alexandrovitch, they say you need rest.

(She pouts)

IVOLGIN
My dear. My dear.

VARYA
Come away, mother!

NINA
I'll see this through to the end.

GANYA
(To Myshkin) Get him away somehow. This is horrible.
Please. Oh, the bitch!

NASTASYA
Are you retired, General?

IVOLGIN
Yes. And in disgrace. Ever since the scandal two years ago
on the railway about a lap dog.

NASTASYA
What was it? And on the railway, too. Let me see, I
think...but tell me about it.

IVOLGIN
Oh, it was a stupid affair, not worth repeating. It was all
about Prince Byelokonsky's governess' mistress,
Schmidt—

NASTASYA
You must tell me!

FERDYSHTCHENKO
I've never heard it before. C'est du nouveau.

VARYA
(Desperately) Father, there's someone to see you.

IVOLGIN
It's a very simple story. I was on my way to Moscow on a very important affair. I sat in one of the compartments smoking my cigar. I was there first, mind you. After a while two ladies with a lap dog seated themselves opposite me. The window was open and there were many other compartments. I paid them little attention beyond noting they were attractive. But suddenly I realized they were staring at me. And in no friendly way. One of them quizzed me with her lorgnette.

Then, without any warning at all the other one took the cigar out of my mouth and hurled it out the window. A savage woman, savage. I was infuriated. But I managed to be a gentleman. I smiled. I bowed courteously, picked up the lap dog and sent it after the cigar.

NASTASYA
(Clapping her hands) You are a monster.

FERDYSHTCHENKO
Bravo, bravo.

NASTASYA
And what did the lady do?

IVOLGIN
She smiled sweetly and without the slightest warning brought her handbag down on my head. Quite a savage type.

NASTASYA
And you?

IVOLGIN

I shook my fist at her, that's all. And then, do you know, she insisted I struck her. That wouldn't have been so bad had it not turned out that she was some sort of friend of Princess Byelokonsky and the other one was the Princess's eldest daughter. I have been a social outcast ever since.

NASTASYA

But this is quite a coincidence. I read the very same story in the Independent a week ago. Only it happened between a Frenchman and an Englishman. Even to the details.

(Only Ferdyshtchenko laughs)

IVOLGIN

(Pale) I assure you the very same thing happened to me.

NASTASYA

What, exactly the same? At two ends of the continent? Fancy that!

IVOLGIN

(Hoarsely) But note that the incident occurred to me two years ago.

(A doorbell rings)

NASTASYA

(Convulsed) Ah, there is that.

GANYA

Father, I beg you to come out and let me have a word with you.

(Enter Rogozhin and Lebedyev and some ruffians)

(Rogozhin's voice is heard from the outside)

ROGOZHIN'S VOICE
I'll just announce myself.

(Enter Rogozhin)

ROGOZHIN
Ah, here he is, the Judas. How are you, Ganya, you scoundrel?

LEBEDYEV
Here he is. Here he is himself.

ROGOZHIN
You didn't expect Parfyon Rogozhin, did you?

(Suddenly sees Nastasya) Then, it's true. Well, you shall pay for this!

(But the presence of the other ladies disconcerts him. Then he spots Myshkin) What! Are you here, too, Prince?

GANYA
But what do you want? This isn't a stable. My mother and sister are here.

ROGOZHIN
We see them.

LEBEDYEV
Yes, note that we see them.

GANYA
Look, just who are you?

ROGOZHIN
He doesn't remember.

LEBEDYEV
He doesn't remember.

ROGOZHIN
Don't you know Rogozhin? Why it's hardly six months since I lost two hundred rubles to you and your cheating friends. But never mind that. I've got lots more money now. I can buy and sell you. You'll crawl on hands and knees. Nastasya Fillipovna, don't turn me away. Tell me: are you going to marry him?

NASTASYA
Certainly not! And what has put it into your head to ask such a question?

ROGOZHIN
But they told me you were engaged to him. To him! As if it were possible.

(Delighted) I told them it was impossible. Ah, this is wonderful. I can buy and sell him. I can buy him off for a thousand rubles. That's right, isn't it, Ganya? You scoundrel. You'd take it, wouldn't you? Or isn't it enough? Here. I came to get you to sign the agreement to do it. Name your price.

GANYA
Get out of this house, you drunk.

(Lebedyev whispers to Rogozhin)

ROGOZHIN
That's right. Here are eighteen thousand rubles, Nastasya. Be mine. There.

(He tosses them to her) And there's more to come.

LEBEDYEV
No, no, no. You're going about this the wrong way.

ROGOZHIN
Quiet fool, I—

(He looks at Nastasya) It seems you are right. I am a fool.

NASTASYA
Eighteen thousand to me? Ah, one can see that he is a peasant.

ROGOZHIN
Forty thousand, then forty. Cash down.

NASTASYA
The bourgeois gentleman.

ROGOZHIN
A hundred then! I've give you a hundred thousand today!

LEBEDYEV
You are mad! You are mad! They'll send for the police and then where will you be?

NASTASYA
He is drunk and boasting.

ROGOZHIN
I'll have it before evening. Get it for me, Lebedyev.

(To Nastasya) I'll show you that I won't stick at anything.

IVOLGIN
(Rising thunderously) What is the meaning of this!

ROGOZHIN
Whom have we here? Come along, old fellow, I'll buy you

a drink.

IVOLGIN
You will? I like brandy you know.

ROGOZHIN
Then it will be brandy. Napoleon brandy for the general.

VARYA
This is too disgusting! Is there no one among you who will take this shameless woman away?

NASTASYA
She calls me a shameless woman. And I came here like a fool to invite them to my party this evening. Is that how you let your sister treat me, Ganya?

GANYA
(Grabbing Varya's arm) What have you done?

VARYA
Let go of me!

GANYA
Apologize! Apologize to her.

VARYA
Let go of me.

(She twists, but cannot get free)

GANYA
You will apologize.

(Varya spits in his face)

NASTASYA
What a girl. Bravo! I congratulate you.

(Ganya is about to pulverize Varya when Myshkin steps in)

MYSHKIN
That's enough

GANYA
(Slapping him) So you're always going to get in my way, are you?

NINA
My God, my God.

MYSHKIN
You may hit me, but not her.

(Suddenly he moves away) How ashamed you will be of what you've done.

(He covers his face, the party crowds around him) I'm all right.

ROGOZHIN
Ah, he will regret it. You will be ashamed, Ganya, for having insulted such a gentle—lamb. Prince, drop them, curse them. Come along—I'll show you what a friend Rogozhin can be.

NASTASYA
I certainly have seen your face somewhere.

MYSHKIN
Aren't you ashamed? Surely you are not what you pretend to be now?

NASTASYA
I really am not like this. He is right.

(She goes out and says something to Nina, then kisses her hand)

(Ganya rushes after her)

NASTASYA
Don't come with me! Good-bye till this evening. You must come, do you hear?

(She goes)

ROGOZHIN
You've lost the game, Ganya.

(He goes out, followed by his gang)

VARYA
(To Myshkin) How is it she obeyed you?

MYSHKIN
In what way?

VARYA
You said she wasn't like that. Yes, you're right, she isn't. But then why did she do it? And why did she stop?

(Nina and Ferdyshtchenko help the General out)

GANYA
Prince, I behaved like a scoundrel. Forgive me, please.

MYSHKIN
I had no idea you were capable of this.

GANYA
Of owning my fault...yes, I think I am.

MYSHKIN

(Pointing to Varya) Here is one whose pardon you ought to ask too.

GANYA

No, they're all my enemies. They never forgive.

VARYA

I will forgive you.

GANYA

And will you go to the party tonight?

VARYA

If you insist. Judge for yourself if it's wise for me to do so.

GANYA

She's not like this you know. It's her tricks.

VARYA

I know that. But she was laughing at you, all the same. It isn't worth the bother, it really isn't.

GANYA

They think I don't know it isn't worth it.

MYSHKIN

You don't have to go through with it.

GANYA

Now I do. After this. Before I was hesitating.

MYSHKIN

It surprises me—

GANYA

Why?

MYSHKIN
Your confidence that Nastasya Fillipovna will marry you.

GANYA
She will.

MYSHKIN
And the money?

GANYA
I'll get it.

MYSHKIN
Why are you so sure?

GANYA
Because that's the arrangement with—Totsky.

MYSHKIN
Totsky—her paramour.

GANYA
"Keeper" is the word, I believe. You know, if I were more of a hypocrite I should have snared her easily. If I'd sweetened the pill she would have believed I loved her. All I had to do was talk about the rights of women and all that balderdash. Or how she shouldn't have one mistake held against her. But I didn't. I made it clear. I make no secret I'm marrying her for her money. And how she hates me because I won't play games with her.

MYSHKIN
Can you have loved her until today?

GANYA
At first. But that's enough! Once we are married, she'll behave quietly. And so will I. But if she proves mutinous, I'll abandon her and take the money with me. I will not be

ridiculous.

MYSHKIN
Yet why should she step into the trap when she sees what misery it will mean for her?

GANYA
Perhaps she wants to be trapped. Perhaps she loves me in her own way.

MYSHKIN
Still, you could find many a wealthy girl who—

GANYA
After this? Hardly! I'm a scoundrel but now the important thing is to persevere.

(Pause) Ah, one thing. I thought you were rather taken with Nastasya Fillipovna.

MYSHKIN
Yes, I like her.

GANYA
Not in love by any chance?

MYSHKIN
N-no.

GANYA
But he is embarrassed. Oh, well. I assure you she is a girl of virtuous life now. You imagine she is living with Totsky? Not for ever so long. You may pay your addresses without fear. Well, I'm off to arrange things.

MYSHKIN
Wait!

GANYA
Yes?

MYSHKIN
When she invited everyone to the party did that include me?

GANYA
You wish to go?

MYSHKIN
Yes—I have an object—

GANYA
Well then come, I'll arrange matters.

(EXIT)

CURTAIN

ACT I

Scene 3

Fillipovna's elegant drawing room later that night.

(A party is in progress)

EPANCHIN
He's innocent. He will amuse us.

FERDYSHTCHENKO
Especially as he has invited himself.

EPANCHIN
And what of that?

FERDYSHTCHENKO
Why he must pay for his entrance then.

EPANCHIN
Unlike you.

FERDYSHTCHENKO
Spare me, General. I am here in a special position.

EPANCHIN
What special position are you in?

FERDYSHTCHENKO
Why, everyone has wit except me. To make up for the de-

fect, I ask leave to speak the truth. Only witless people do so. I am only kept and received so that I may talk in this manner. Can such a person as I be received in the same company with a gentleman like yourself and Mr. Totsky?

EPANCHIN
You're talking nonsense again.

(Nastasya laughs)

FERDYSHTCHENKO
The Prince will begin by singing us a popular song.

NASTASYA
(Dryly) I don't think so, and please don't get excited....

FERDYSHTCHENKO
Ah! If he is under special protection, I will be indulged, too.

A FOOTMAN
Prince Myshkin.

NASTASYA
(Going to him) I am sorry that I forgot to invite you earlier. And I'm very glad you've come.

MYSHKIN
I had such a longing to see you that I—forgive me.

NASTASYA
Don't ask forgiveness. That would ruin everything.

MYSHKIN
You are so perfect!

NASTASYA
You think so, do you? You are mistaken. I'll remind you

of that later. Come let me introduce you. I believe the only person you don't know is Mr. Totsky.

TOTSKY
I am delighted, Prince.

MYSHKIN
You are very kind.

EPANCHIN
Buy why has he come?

GANYA
That's clear enough. He took one look at Nastasya Fillipovna and come he must. Besides, he confessed himself to me.

MYSHKIN
I've made you no confession. I simply answered your question.

FERDYSHTCHENKO
Bravo, bravo! That's sincere—and sly, too.

TOTSKY
Don't shout, Ferdyshtchenko.

EPANCHIN
One wouldn't have expected such enterprise from you, Prince. Why, I looked on you as a philosopher.

FERDYSHTCHENKO
And judging from the way the Prince blushes, he is cherishing only the most honorable intentions.

NASTASYA
What time is it?

GANYA
Half past ten.

NASTASYA
It is early yet. Shall we have some champagne?

FERDYSHTCHENKO
This party is dead. I suggest we liven it up a bit. I know an excellent game.

NASTASYA
Well?

FERDYSHTCHENKO
Each one tells the most reprehensible act of his or her life. No lying. It will break the ice a bit. Everyone feels a bit superior to anyone else. This way we all learn each others' foibles.

TOTSKY
Ridiculous. It's just a form of bragging.

NASTASYA
That's just what's wanted, Count.

(Eagerly) You see it really would be nice, volunteering of course. We really aren't very lively.

TOTSKY
What if it's something that can't be told before ladies?

FERDYSHTCHENKO
Why, don't you tell it then? There are plenty of other stories.

MYSHKIN
But I don't know which of my actions I consider the worst.

GANYA
What proof is there I shan't tell lies?

FERDYSHTCHENKO
Well it's fascinating to see what lies a man will tell. But there's no worry about you, Ganya, for we all know, your most reprehensible action.

TOTSKY
Are you really in earnest, Nastasya?

NASTASYA
If you are afraid of wolves, you mustn't go into the forest.

TOTSKY
But telling the truth is in the worst possible taste.

FERDYSHTCHENKO
I'll start. Tell me, do you think a person can steal and not be a thief? I assure I have stolen, but I am not a thief. It happened the year before last. I asked the daughter of Semyon Ivanovitch to play the piano. She got up from where she was sitting and obliged me. On her table was a three-ruble note. I pocketed it.

GANYA
Why?

FERDYSHTCHENKO
I have no idea.

GANYA
Were you suspected?

FERDYSHTCHENKO
No, but the maid was. Do you know? I preached to her and tried to persuade her to confess. Later that night I spent the money on very expensive wine to celebrate. I felt abso-

lutely no guilt about it. Still don't.

NASTASYA
There's no doubt it's the worst thing you've ever done.

TOTSKY
That's a pathological incident, not an action.

NASTASYA
And the servant?

FERDYSHTCHENKO
Turned away the next day, of course.

NASTASYA
And you let that happen?

FERDYSHTCHENKO
You couldn't expect me to peach on myself, could you?

NASTASYA
How loathsome!

FERDYSHTCHENKO
Well, what do you expect? A man's worst actions are always loathsome. General, your turn.

EPANCHIN
I've done some pretty nasty things but the one I'm going to tell about is easily the basest. It happened a long time ago when I was a mere ensign! My orderly and I were staying with an old lady who kept house for us. One day she stole a cock of mine. The matter was never cleared up but she was the only one who could have done it. First chance we got we moved. However, we forgot to take our kitchen pot and we had nothing to cook our soup in. She refused to give it back to my orderly because she claimed we had broken one of her pots. I was boiling. I went back

and gave her a piece of my mind. She as sitting on the stoop and made no answer. Suddenly, I realized she was dead. The whole thing shook me badly. I wasn't able to forget about it until about ten years ago when I endowed an almshouse for indigent women.

FERDYSHTCHENKO
That's cheating. You've told us your best action.

NASTASYA
Yes, General. I never imagined you had such a good heart. I am disappointed.

EPANCHIN
Can't be helped. Your turn, Totsky.

NASTASYA
No, it's my turn. Tell me, Prince—my old friends here want me to be married. What do you think? Shall I be married or not? As you say I will do.

MYSHKIN
To whom?

NASTASYA
To Ganya.

MYSHKIN
No, don't marry him.

NASTASYA
So be it. Ganya, you have heard the Prince's decision? Well, that's my answer, once and for all.

TOTSKY
Nastasya Fillipovna!

EPANCHIN
Dear girl—

NASTASYA
Why what is the matter? How distressed you all look!

TOTSKY
But you promised quite voluntarily and to break it like this—before people.

NASTASYA
Before people? I don't understand you. Aren't we in the company of intimate friends? You heard me tell the Prince I would abide his decision. If he had said yes, I would have given my consent at once. My whole life was hanging in the balance. What could be more serious?

EPANCHIN
What has the Prince to do with it? And what is the Prince after all?

NASTASYA
He is only a man I have met in my whole life that I believe is my sincere friend.

GANYA
I have only to thank Nastasya Fillipovna for the extraordinary delicacy with which she had treated me. But the Prince, the Prince is—

NASTASYA
—Is after the seventy-five thousand, do you mean? Don't deny it. You certainly meant to say it. And, dear, Count, I forgot to add, take back that money. I set you free for nothing. It's time you were free. Nine years and three months. Tomorrow a new leaf; but today is my birthday, and I am doing what I like for the first time in my whole life. Tomorrow I shall leave this flat for good, and there

will be no more parties, friends.

(She jumps up)

EPANCHIN AND TOTSKY
Nastasya Fillipovna! Nastasya Fillipovna!

(A violent ring of the bell)

NASTASYA
Ah. Here's a way out. It's time at last. I beg you be seated, friends.

FERDYSHTCHENKO
Rogozhin and his hundred thousand, not a doubt of it.

(The maid enters)

KATYA
There's a dozen men here and they're all drunk. They say it's Rogozhin and that you know.

NASTASYA
That's right, Katya, show them all in at once.

KATYA
Not all of them. They're in a disgraceful state. Shocking.

NASTASYA
Let them all in, Katya. Don't be afraid or they'll come in without your showing. What a commotion they are making. Perhaps you are offended, friends, at my receiving such company in your presence? I am very sorry and I beg your pardon. I am very, very anxious that you should witness this final scene—

EPANCHIN
I am afraid that my position will not—

NASTASYA
Of course. I hadn't thought of that, but I wanted you to be beside me at this moment.

EPANCHIN
Then from devotion to you, dear lady—I will stay. But I advise you to reconsider.

FERDYSHTCHENKO
Rogozhin himself.

(They all enter)

EPANCHIN
(To Totsky) What do you think, Count? Hasn't she taken leave of her senses? I mean not allegorically but in the literal, medical sense.

TOTSKY
She's always been disposed that way.

LEBEDYEV
(Stepping forward, extending a package to Nastasya) Here!

NASTASYA
What's this?

ROGOZHIN
(Gasping) A hundred thousand.

NASTASYA
So, he's kept his word! What a man! Sit down please. I shall have something to say to you later. Well, have your friends sit down. There are plenty of arm chairs.

(The embarrassed ruffians do sit down) What's the matter with them? Don't they want to?

(Holding up bundle) This, friends, is a hundred thousand rubles. This afternoon he shouted like a madman that he would bring me a hundred thousand this evening and I've been expecting him all the time. He was bidding for me. He's kept his word. It all happened at Ganya's this afternoon. I went to pay a visit to his mother in my future home and there his sister wanted to turn me out. She spat in her brother's face. She is a girl of character.

EPANCHIN
Nastasya!

NASTASYA
What's the matter, General? Is it improper to tell the truth? Let's give up the humbugging. What good has it done me to behave like a virtuous woman for five years. I've been a silly fool. Rogozhin has ended all that. He comes in and lays his money down on the table. Ganya, I see you are still angry. Could you really have meant to make me one of your family? Me, Rogozhin's woman? What did the Prince say just now?

MYSHKIN
I didn't say you were Rogozhin's woman. You don't belong to him.

NASTASYA
I simply can't understand what possessed me to enter an honorable family. I wanted to see how far you'd go and you really surprised me. I expected a great deal but not that. Is Rogozhin right when he said you'd crawl on all fours for three rubles?

ROGOZHIN
Yes, he would, too!

NASTASYA
It would be different if you were starving. But why bring a

wife you hate into your house? Yes. I do believe you'd murder for money. As for that bouquet holder

(She indicates Epanchin) I say nothing.

EPANCHIN
Is this you? Is this you, Nastasya? You, so refined, with such delicate ideas?

NASTASYA
This is my day, General. I would have my fling! My red-letter day. I've been waiting for a long time. And look at Count Totsky, laughing.

TOTSKY
I'm not laughing. I am listening with the greatest attention.

NASTASYA
Why have I been tormenting him for the last five years and not letting him go? He has kept me like a countess. He even sought me out a respectable husband. Would you believe it I have not lived with him the last five years and yet I've taken his money as though I had a right to it? I've been completely lost to all sense. And do you know I might have married? And not Ganya, either. I might have married the Count, for spite. He would have. He urged it himself. He was lying, of course. But he's easily tempted and can't restrain himself. But he wasn't worth the anger. I'd better be in my proper place: in the streets. I'm leaving and taking nothing with me. Who'll take anyone with nothing? Ask Ganya if he'll have me! Why even Ferdy-shtchenko wouldn't.

FERDYSHTCHENKO
Perhaps Ferdyshtchenko wouldn't. You see I am a candid person. But the Prince would take you. Ask him.

NASTASYA
Is that true?

MYSHKIN
It's true.

NASTASYA
As I am, with nothing?

MYSHKIN
I will, Nastasya Fillipovna.

EPANCHIN
Here's a new development. I might have expected it.

NASTASYA
Here's a find. And simply from goodness of heart, too, I have found. What are you going to live on, if you are so in love that you, a Prince, are ready to marry Rogozhin's woman?

MYSHKIN
I am going to marry an honest woman, not Rogozhin's woman.

NASTASYA
You think I am honest?

MYSHKIN
Yes.

NASTASYA
That's an old fashioned fancy. Nowadays the world has grown wiser.

MYSHKIN
No—I consider you will be doing me an honor, not I, you. You have suffered and come out of that hell. Why then are

you ashamed and ready to go? You have given back the money. No one else would do that. Nastasya, I love you. I would die for you. If we are poor, I'd work.

(Sniggers from Lebedyev and Ferdyshtchenko)

MYSHKIN
But, perhaps, we shan't be poor, but very rich. I don't know for certain. I had a letter from Mr. Salazakin that informed me I may receive a very large inheritance.

(Silence)

EPANCHIN
He's raving. This is a perfect madhouse.

TOTSKY
You say Salazakin? He is well known to me. A very reputable lawyer. I know his handwriting if you would let me have a look at it. I might tell you.

EPANCHIN
What next? What next?

TOTSKY
It's genuine. By uncontested will of your aunt you will inherit a large fortune without any difficulty.

EPANCHIN
Impossible!

TOTSKY
You can take Salazakin's word as gospel. I congratulate you. You are now worth at least two million rubles—possibly more.

FERDYSHTCHENKO
Bravo! The last of the Myshkins.

LEBEDYEV
Hurrah!

EPANCHIN
It's a fairy tale, that's what it is. Well, I congratulate you—I congratulate you.

NASTASYA
Then I am really a Princess? It's a surprise ending. But why are you all standing, friends? I think someone asked for champagne. Katya, come here. I am going to be married. Did you hear? To the Prince. He has two millions, he is Prince Myshkin and he is marrying me.

KATYA
And a good thing too, my lady; it's high time. It's not a chance to miss.

NASTASYA
Sit down beside me, Prince. That's right. And here they are with the wine. Congratulate us friends!

FERDYSHTCHENKO
Hurrah!

LEBEDYEV
This is not so extraordinary; Princes have married gypsies.

EPANCHIN
Prince, consider what you are doing.

NASTASYA
No, General! I am a Princess now, do you hear? The Prince won't let me be insulted. Count, congratulate me, too. I can sit beside your wife now everywhere. It's a good bargain, a husband like that? Two millions and a Prince and an idiot too? Rogozhin. I've made a better arrangement.

ROGOZHIN
Give her up!

KATYA
For you? He's going to marry her.

ROGOZHIN
I'll marry her, too. I'll marry her at once, this minute. I'll give up everything.

KATYA
Drunkard!

NASTASYA
Do you hear, Prince? That's how a peasant bids for your bride.

MYSHKIN
He is drunk. He loves you very much.

NASTASYA
How can you marry a woman who almost went off with that...peasant?

MYSHKIN
You were in a fever. You're in a fever now. Almost delirious—

NASTASYA
And won't you feel ashamed when people tell you afterwards that your wife was a kept woman?

MYSHKIN
No—I shan't be ashamed. It wasn't your doing.

NASTASYA
And you will never reproach me with it?

MYSHKIN
Never!

NASTASYA
Be careful. Don't answer for your whole life.

MYSHKIN
Nastasya, why dwell on it? You wanted to ruin yourself irrevocably. But you are not to blame for anything. What does it matter what Rogozhin or Ganya do? You are proud, Nastasya, and, perhaps, foolish enough to blame yourself. You want looking after, Nastasya, and I will look after you. I shall respect you all my life.

TOTSKY
He is an idiot! But he knows that flattery is the best way to get at people. It's sheer instinct.

EPANCHIN
Poor fellow.

NASTASYA
Thank you, Prince. No one has ever talked to me like that before. They've all tried to buy me. But no decent man has ever thought of marrying me. Did you hear that, Count? What do you think of what the Prince said? It was almost improper, don't you think? Rogozhin, don't go away yet! But you are not going, I see. Perhaps I shall come with you after all. Where do you mean to take me?

ROGOZHIN
To Moscow.

MYSHKIN
Nastasya—

NASTASYA
Did you really think I meant it? Ruin a child like that?

That's more in the Count's line: he is fond of children.

TOTSKY
Nastasya!

NASTASYA
Come along, Rogozhin! Get your money ready. Never mind about wanting to marry me, let me have the money all the same. Perhaps I shan't marry you after all. You thought if you married me you'd save money? Not very likely. I'm a whore, Totsky's whore. Don't forget that!

ROGOZHIN
There's no need to—

NASTASYA
You ought to marry General Epanchin's daughter now, Prince. Not me. I won't ruin you. You don't think so now but you would reproach me afterwards; and I couldn't bear that.

MYSHKIN
I would never reproach you.

NASTASYA
Which would be worse. For then I would reproach myself. Come along, Rogozhin!

MYSHKIN
Is it possible?

NASTASYA
Did you think I meant it? I am proud, as you say. Simply for the pride of being able to boast of rejecting a Prince, I am going into the gutter. What sort of wife would I make you? And look at poor Ganya! He won't get your money now, Count. But I'll comfort you, Ganya, myself! Come on, Rogozhin, let's go.

ROGOZHIN
Let's go. Hey, Lebedyev, get ready the wine.

NASTASYA
Have plenty of wine ready. I want to drink. And there will be music.

ROGOZHIN
Yes, yes. Don't go near her. She's mine! All mine. My queen. Don't come near her. Don't come near her.

NASTASYA
Why are you bellowing? I can still kick you out. I can if I choose. I haven't taken your money yet. Give it here. Is there a hundred thousand in it?

ROGOZHIN
Yes. Yes. I assure you.

NASTASYA
Look, Prince, look! See what a whore your betrothed is. You should laugh. The General wants you for his daughter. A much better bargain. Why are you crying, Prince? You should laugh as I do.

(She is not laughing) It is better so, Prince. It is better so. We should not have been happy. You are right, we've met before. In my dreams. I've always dreamt of someone like you. Some kind and good and honest *and* so stupid he wouldn't let me see me for what I am. I used to dream like that until I nearly went out of my mind. Rogozhin, are you ready?

ROGOZHIN
Ready. Don't come near her.

LEBEDYEV
The troikas are ready with bells.

NASTASYA
Ganya, I want to compensate you. Why should you lose everything? Rogozhin would he crawl on all fours for three rubles?

ROGOZHIN
He would.

NASTASYA
Then listen, Ganya; I want to see into your soul for the last time. You've been torturing me, now it's my turn. You see this roll? There are a hundred thousand rubles. I'm going to throw it in the fire. Now if you can pull it out, bare-handed, no tongs, it's yours. You'll burn your fingers a little but it's a hundred thousand and I shall admire your spirit. If you don't it will burn. I won't let anyone else touch it. It's my money! It's my wages for a night with Rogozhin. Is it my money, Rogozhin?

ROGOZHIN
Yours, yours, my queen!

NASTASYA
Then stand back. I may do what I like.

EPANCHIN
She's out of her mind—completely. Oughtn't we to tie her up?

TOTSKY
I told you she is a woman of glaring effects. An alluring woman!

LEBEDYEV
Madame! Royal lady! Omnipotent lady!

(He is on his knees) Tell me to pick them out. I'll get right in. I have thirteen children—all of them orphans.

(He tries to get in the fire)

NASTASYA
Get away! All stand back! Ganya, why are you standing still? Don't be shy. Pick it out. If you don't you'll hang yourself afterward.

LEBEDYEV
Lady!

(He rushes forward, only to be clouted by Rogozhin)

ROGOZHIN
That's like my queen. That's style. Which of you pickpockets would do a thing like that?

FERDYSHTCHENKO
I'd pull it out with my teeth for a paltry thousand.

LEBEDYEV
It's burning! It's on fire!

FERDYSHTCHENKO
Pick it out!

NASTASYA
Ganya, don't show off. For the last time, I say...

FERDYSHTCHENKO
Pull it out! Pull it out, you concerted jackanapes. It'll be burned. Oh, damn you!

LEBEDYEV
Dear lady, it will be burned.

(Ganya walks out of the room, Nastasya pulls the money out with the tongs)

LEBEDYEV
Only a poor little thousand spoilt.

NASTASYA
It's all his! He wouldn't do it, so his vanity is even greater than his greed. Rogozhin, march! Goodbye, Prince. You are the first man I have seen in my life. Goodbye, Count, merci.

(Myshkin rushes after her)

EPANCHIN
Pray, think what you are doing, Prince! Give it up. I speak as a father.

(The Prince has gone)

MYSHKIN'S VOICE
To Moscow! Follow the troikas!

EPANCHIN
I am sorry—genuinely, sorry. She is a lost woman. But the Prince isn't for her now. He's too good a match. Now, I have a daughter....

TOTSKY
Amongst the Japanese, they say anyone who has received an insult goes to his enemy and cuts open his stomach before him. I never saw the point before. Ah, she is a woman of great effects. An alluring woman—alluring.

CURTAIN

ACT II

Scene 4

In this act the Prince's circumstances have obviously improved. But he is still awkward and shy and deferential. Only his clothes are better.

Rogozhin's palace. A knock. Rogozhin himself answers it. He stops and stares at Myshkin.

MYSHKIN
Parfyon, perhaps I've come at the wrong moment. I can go away, you know.

ROGOZHIN
Not at all, not at all. Come in. You are welcome. Why do you stare so? Sit down.

MYSHKIN
Did you know that I was coming today or not?

ROGOZHIN
I thought so, I was right. But how could I tell for sure?

MYSHKIN
Why be so cross about it?

ROGOZHIN
Why do you ask?

MYSHKIN
Even as I got out of the train this morning, I saw two eyes that looked at me just like you did.

ROGOZHIN
You don't say. Whose eyes were they?

MYSHKIN
I don't know. I felt almost sweat pouring over me, as I did when I had fits five years ago.

ROGOZHIN
Well, perhaps, it was your fancy, I don't know.

MYSHKIN
Perhaps. Are you settled here for good?

ROGOZHIN
Yes, I am home. Where else should I be?

MYSHKIN
It's been a long time since we met. I've heard such things about you, not like yourself.

ROGOZHIN
People will say anything.

MYSHKIN
You've turned off all your followers.

ROGOZHIN
(Morosely) Yes.

MYSHKIN
(Embarrassed) I guessed it was your house from quite a distance.

ROGOZHIN
How was that?

MYSHKIN
Before I had an idea that you lived in such a house. When I saw it, I knew it must be yours. It's so dark. You are living here in darkness. Is that your father?

(Pointing to a portrait)

ROGOZHIN
Yes, it is.

MYSHKIN
He wasn't one of the Old Believers, was he?

ROGOZHIN
No. Why do you ask?

MYSHKIN
Will you have your wedding here?

ROGOZHIN
Yes.

MYSHKIN
Will it be soon?

ROGOZHIN
You know yourself that doesn't depend on me.

MYSHKIN
Parfyon, I am not your enemy. I won't interfere with you in any way. When she fled from you in Moscow and came to me and asked me to save her from you, we lived apart.

ROGOZHIN
All that time? A full month?

MYSHKIN
You know it. I came here with a purpose. I wish to persuade her to go abroad—for her health. I don't mean to accompany her. She is ill, Rogozhin, and needs care. I have never concealed from you that I have always felt it would be better for both of you to part. But since you have made it up I will go without seeing her. You said you understood how I felt once. But here you are looking at me with hatred. I will go now and I won't come back.

(He rises)

ROGOZHIN
Stay with me a little. It's a long time since I've seen you.

(He holds his head on his hands) When you are not here, I hate you. But you haven't been sitting here ten minutes when you are as dear to me as ever. Stay with me a little.

MYSHKIN
You believe me when I am with you?

ROGOZHIN
I believe your voice. Later, I will suspect your words. I understand, of course, that we can't be put on a level—you and I.

MYSHKIN
Why do you add that? Now you are irritated again.

ROGOZHIN
Our opinion is not asked in the matter. It's settled. You see we love in different ways. You say you love her with pity. There's no pity for her in me. And she hates me, too, more than anything. Would you believe it, I haven't seen her for five days because I don't dare? She'll ask me "What have you come for?" She has covered me with shame.

MYSHKIN
Shame? How can you?

ROGOZHIN
Though you didn't know, she ran away to you on our wedding day—

MYSHKIN
But you yourself know—

ROGOZHIN
Didn't she shame me in Moscow with that Hussar? I know for certain she did. And even after she had fixed the wedding day.

MYSHKIN
Impossible!

ROGOZHIN
I know it for a fact. She's not that type you say? Not with you. But with me, yes. I know for a fact that simply to make a laughingstock of me—oh, the tricks she played me in Moscow!

MYSHKIN
And you are marrying her now? What will you do later?

ROGOZHIN
It's five days since I've been with her. She keeps telling me that I don't own her. Sometimes, it's true, she only does this to scare me. She is always laughing at me somehow. But sometimes she is really sullen and won't say a word. I give her presents and she gives them to her maid. I watch her house. She knows it. She asks me what I would do if I caught her with another man. She doesn't have to ask. I couldn't stand it. She knows.

MYSHKIN
What does she know?

ROGOZHIN
How do I know? I've never been able to catch her. In Moscow I was always on her track. I told her what she was one day.

MYSHKIN
You told her?

ROGOZHIN
Yes.

MYSHKIN
Well?

ROGOZHIN
She said she'd never marry me. She wouldn't even take me for her lackey. I beat her black and blue.

MYSHKIN
Don't you see you can't go on this way?

ROGOZHIN
Who better than I? She wouldn't forgive me though I begged her on my knees. She went out with all her friends and laughed at me. She came back alone. She said they were all cowards and afraid of me. But she laughed, she wasn't afraid. She went to bed and didn't even lock the door. I couldn't sleep. I couldn't eat. The next morning she laughed at me but she was friendly enough. She asked me if I would punish her once I married her. I told her the truth: I didn't know. She didn't even regard me worth her anger. Later, she said she'd marry me. Do you know why? Because it was as good a way as any to ruin herself. Then she fixed the day and a week later she ran off to Lebedyev. When I found her, she said she wanted to wait a while.

That's how we stand now—what do you think of all that? What do you think of it yourself?

MYSHKIN
What do you think of it yourself?

ROGOZHIN
Do you suppose I think?

MYSHKIN
I won't hinder you in any way.

ROGOZHIN
How is it that you give in to me like this? Have you quite got over loving her? You used to be miserable anyway. I saw that. Why have you come here? From pity?

MYSHKIN
You think I am deceiving you?

ROGOZHIN
No, I believe you. It's just that I can't make it out. Is your pity greater than my love?

MYSHKIN
There's no distinguishing your love from hate. It will pass then and, perhaps, the trouble will be worse. I tell you this, brother—

ROGOZHIN
That I shall murder her.

MYSHKIN
You hate her bitterly for this love, for all this torture you are suffering. Why does she go through with it? Any man would be better because—because you really may murder her, Rogozhin, and she knows that only too well by now. Is it because you love her so passionately? That may be it.

There are women who want just that sort of love—only.

ROGOZHIN
Why are you smiling at my father's portrait?

MYSHKIN
It struck me that if it hadn't been for this love you would have become exactly like your father. You would have lived a quiet life, heaping up money.

ROGOZHIN
Laugh away; but do you know she said the very same thing not long ago. It's queer how you both say the same thing.

MYSHKIN
She has been here?

ROGOZHIN
Yes. She stood there and looked at the portrait. She told me I was headstrong, passionate, and if it weren't for my intelligence, I'd go to Siberia. Can you imagine? It's the first time she had ever spoken to me so. She saw some books and told me I should educate myself. She said she'd prepare me a list of books to read. It was the first time she ever talked to me like that. For the first time I breathed like a living man.

MYSHKIN
Perhaps God will bring you together.

ROGOZHIN
That will never be.

MYSHKIN
Don't be without hope. Surely if she marries you, she will see your good qualities. If that were not so it would be as foolish as to deliberately drown herself, or tempt murder.

ROGOZHIN
That's just why she's marrying me! Just why! Because she expects to be murdered. Do you pretend not to understand what's at the root of it?

MYSHKIN
I don't understand you.

ROGOZHIN
Well, perhaps, you really don't. They say you are not quite right. She loves another man just as I love her. And do you know who he is? It's you.

MYSHKIN
Me?

ROGOZHIN
You. She's loved you ever since that day. She's told me so. But she won't marry you. She won't ruin you. She keeps saying she won't disgrace you. But it doesn't matter. She can marry me.

MYSHKIN
But why did she run away from me then?

ROGOZHIN
And back and forth and back and forth? All sorts of ideas come to her, poor thing. She cries, she laughs. She ran away from you because she loved you. She was trying to be noble. She doesn't think she's worthy. She would have drowned herself long ago if it weren't for me. You know why? Because I am more dreadful than the water. She marries me from spite—from spite!

MYSHKIN
How can you do it then?

ROGOZHIN
You're thinking you must prevent it?

MYSHKIN
I didn't come here with that idea.

ROGOZHIN
But you have it now. Well that's enough.

(He is toying with a knife)

MYSHKIN
It's all jealousy. It's sick. What are you doing?

ROGOZHIN
Leave it alone.

MYSHKIN
I had a premonition of all this. I wanted to root it out of my heart, Rogozhin, but it's not so easy. Well, goodbye. But what are you doing?

(Myshkin has picked up the knife, but Rogozhin snatches it from him)

MYSHKIN
Do you cut the pages with it?

ROGOZHIN
Yes.

MYSHKIN
But it's a garden knife.

ROGOZHIN
So? Does it matter?

MYSHKIN
But it is quite new.

ROGOZHIN
Why shouldn't I buy a new knife?

MYSHKIN
I'd better go.

(He gets up)

ROGOZHIN
Do you believe in God?

MYSHKIN
What a strange question.

ROGOZHIN
I was looking at that picture.

MYSHKIN
At that picture? It might make one lose one's faith.

ROGOZHIN
That's what it is doing.

MYSHKIN
What do you mean? I was joking. Why did you ask that?

ROGOZHIN
Many people don't believe nowadays.

MYSHKIN
All I know is that a few days ago an atheist was killed by a religious man for his atheism. The religious man prayed to God as he cut his friend's throat. It was an act of piety, you see.

ROGOZHIN
(Laughs) I like that. That beats everything.

MYSHKIN
Yesterday, a drunken soldier sold me a silver cross. Of course, it was made of tin. But I bought it. He was so happy to have cheated me. I let him cheat me. It made him happy.

ROGOZHIN
Have you got it with you?

MYSHKIN
Yes.

ROGOZHIN
Show me. Give it to me.

MYSHKIN
Why? I'd rather....

ROGOZHIN
I'll wear it and give you mine.

MYSHKIN
You want to change crosses? Certainly. We will be brothers.

ROGOZHIN
Don't be afraid. Though I've taken your cross, I won't murder you for your watch.

(He embraces him)

MYSHKIN
Take her then. She's yours. I've given in to you. Remember Rogozhin....

(Myshkin falls into a fit)

ROGOZHIN
Prince, what is wrong? Ah, it's his fit. His fit....

CURTAIN

ACT II

Scene 5

The scene is Lebedyev's garden. There are some trees and a small garden. At the audience's right is the house. At the rear a stone wall with gates is visible. The gates are open. In the center are garden seats and tables. The time is spring.

LEBEDYEV
That monster has been here every morning to ask after your health.

MYSHKIN
Why do you call him a monster?

LEBEDYEV
Because I wish to show that I am no longer on his side and that I am not afraid of him.

MYSHKIN
And why are you always approaching me as if you wanted to whisper a secret in my ear?

LEBEDYEV
I am abject. I feel it. As it happens I do have a secret to tell you. A person you know wishes an interview with you, in secret.

MYSHKIN
Why in secret? I'll go to her today, myself.

LEBEDYEV
Because she is afraid of Aglaia Ivanova.

MYSHKIN
I've forbidden you to mention Aglaia to me. Ever since you've had the ridiculous notion she's in love with me.

LEBEDYEV
It seems Nastasya Fillipovna shares my opinion. It is Nastasya's wish that Aglaia should become your wife.

MYSHKIN
This is absurd.

LEBEDYEV
It is not so absurd. She has written to Aglaia about you.

MYSHKIN
What? I don't believe it.

LEBEDYEV
I've seen the letters. And I believe, but I'm not sure, that Aglaia replies to them.

MYSHKIN
This grows more and more incredible.

(A servant escorts in the Epanchins)

(Enter the servant, General Epanchin, Madame Epanchin, Mademoiselle Epanchin)

This is a delightful surprise.

(The Prince and Lebedyev rush to find the ladies chairs)

MADAME EPANCHIN
Prince, you're very lively. I expected to find you on death's door. I confess, your good health vexes me no end. Are you staying long?

MYSHKIN
Perhaps the whole summer.

MADAME EPANCHIN
You are alone, aren't you? Not married?

AGLAIA
Maman!

MYSHKIN
No, not married.

MADAME EPANCHIN
Why haven't you come to us? Why do you stay with that person? Why does he wriggle about like that?

LEBEDYEV
I am abject, abject. I feel it.

MADAME EPANCHIN
He is mad.

MYSHKIN
No, no.

MADAME EPANCHIN
Drunk like the last time?

(General Ivolgin enters)

IVOLGIN
Good morning, Prince. Ah, who have we here? Aglaia Ivanova. I used to carry you in my arms.

MADAME EPANCHIN
You are lying, sir, as usual.

AGLAIA
You've forgotten, Maman, he really did.

IVOLGIN
Dear me. I did. Fancy that. I used to be a guest in your house, Ivan Fyodorovitch.

MADAME EPANCHIN
And see what you've come to now. You should cry.

(Ivolgin draws himself up to go)

MADAME EPANCHIN
Ardalion Alexandrovitch, my dear man. Stop a minute, we are all sinners. Come see us again.

(Ivolgin goes)

LEBEDYEV
That's what comes of speaking the truth. Tears!

EPANCHIN
Was that Ganya I just saw?

MYSHKIN
Yes. He is my steward now. He has changed much.

MADAME EPANCHIN
Well, his sister hasn't. Do you know she was carrying messages from Ganya to Aglaia?

MYSHKIN
I know he deceives me at times.

MADAME EPANCHIN
Know it and go on trusting him? Oh, why didn't you come to stay with us instead of this Lebedyev!

MYSHKIN
Well, I was forbidden....

MADAME EPANCHIN
When? By whom?

MYSHKIN
By Aglaia.

MADAME EPANCHIN
What!

MYSHKIN
I am not agreeable company for a young lady. My gestures are unsuitable. I've no sense of proportion. My words are incongruous. And so I have no right. It is impossible not to laugh at me sometimes. It is so, isn't it?

AGLAIA
Why do you humble yourself before them? Them! Them! There's no one here worth your little finger. Why have you no pride?

EPANCHIN
Why did you forbid the Prince the house?

AGLAIA
Why do all of you torture me, every one of you? They're all pestering me on your account, Prince. Why? Nothing will induce me to marry you. I never will on any consideration. As though one could marry an absurd creature like you! Why, why do they tease me and say I'm going to marry you? You're in the plot with them, too.

EPANCHIN
No one has ever teased you about it that I know of....

MADAME EPANCHIN
No one has ever thought of such a thing. Who has been teasing her? Is she raving?

AGLAIA
Everyone has been talking about it. Everyone. For the last three days. I will never, never, never marry him.

(She sobs)

EPANCHIN
But he hasn't even....

MYSHKIN
I haven't asked you.

MADAME EPANCHIN
What's that?

MYSHKIN
It's not my fault, Aglaia Ivanova. I never—it never entered my head. Nor shall I ever—

(Aglaia looks at him and laughs hysterically)

MYSHKIN
Well then, it's all right.

MADAME EPANCHIN
Oh dear, she's in love with him. It's worse than I feared.

EPANCHIN
But how can she be in love after that display?

MADAME EPANCHIN
You'll see. Oh, dear.

AGLAIA
You've refused me? You've refused me for good haven't you, Prince? You shan't change your mind?

MYSHKIN
No.

AGLAIA
Then you may give me a kiss.

EPANCHIN
Well, this beats all!

(Ganya enters, to Lebedyev)

GANYA
Why don't you tell him about these people? They'll come in of themselves if you don't. Prince, there are three men to see you, but Lebedyev, here, won't let them in to you.

MYSHKIN
Who are they?

LEBEDYEV
The son of Pavlishtchev and his friends. They are not worth it.

MYSHKIN
The son of Pavlishtchev! Let him in.

AGLAIA
It will be a very good thing if you put a stop to this at once, yourself.

MADAME EPANCHIN
I want this disgusting claim to be stopped at last, too.

MYSHKIN
It seems everyone knows about my affairs.

AGLAIA
It's all over town. They've put out a disgusting pamphlet.

MYSHKIN
Let them in.

(The three boys, all in their teens come in)

ANTIP
Antip Burdovsky, the son of Pavlishtchev.

VLADIMIR
Vladimir Dobtorenko, Mr. Lebedyev's nephew.

LEBEDYEV
I'd like to forget that.

VLADIMIR
I'm not about to let you.

IPPOLIT
Terentyev. Ippolit Terentyev.

MYSHKIN
I did not expect any of you. I asked Ganya to deal with this. However, I have no objection to a personal explanation. If you would step inside, I have my friends here, so if it won't take too long....

VLADIMIR
So many friends as you like, but allow us to point out you might have treated us politely and not left us waiting two

hours in your servants' quarters.

ANTIP
Of course, this is behaving like a Prince, but I am not your servant, I—

IPPOLIT
It was like a Prince.

MYSHKIN
Gentlemen, I only heard this minute you were here.

IPPOLIT
But what right have you to submit this to your friends?

MYSHKIN
But if you'll just step inside—

ANTIP
Anyone can see what their judgment would be. You've no right...your friends...so there!

MADAME EPANCHIN
Here, read this! This is what they circulate about you.

MYSHKIN
It would be better not.

MADAME EPANCHIN
Read it aloud or we shall quarrel.

VLADIMIR
Here, I'll be glad to:

"Proletarians, hear an episode of daily justice. Here is an anecdote of a scion of the nobility whose grandfather was ruined by roulette, whose father had to serve as a sub-lieutenant.

"Our scion wearing gaiters like a foreigner shivered in an unlined coat.

"He returned to Russia from Switzerland where he had been under treatment for idiocy.

"Left a baby at his father's death (a death fortuitously occurring while his father was on trial for scandalous misconduct), he was supported by the charity of a very rich landowner—we will call him P. Until he was twenty the idiot Prince could speak no language, not even his native Russian.

"Suddenly, P died leaving no will, of course. But instead of falling on hard times our hero inherited a fortune from an entirely unexpected source. Our idiot became a very desirable match. An aristocrat, a millionaire, an idiot—what better qualifications for a husband."

EPANCHIN
This passes my comprehension.

MYSHKIN
Leave off.

MADAME EPANCHIN
Read it. Read it. If you stop we shall quarrel.

VLADIMIR
(Continues) "But now a new development. The licentious P had seduced a servant girl in his youth. The result was a son. P cared for them for a while but in the end forgot about them.

"A lawyer approached the Prince on behalf of the son. You think this innocent Prince would want to repay the huge sums expended? Not a bit. 'Do you think I am an idiot?' cries the Prince. 'Here's a hundred rubles.' Of course it was flung back in his face. The Prince was no idiot."

EPANCHIN
This is beyond anything. It is as if a hundred lackeys had composed it.

IPPOLIT
How dare you make such insulting suppositions?

MYSHKIN
Allow me to speak. I say nothing of the article, it's all untrue. I am sure none of you had a hand in it.

IPPOLIT
I knew nothing of the article. I don't approve of the article.

(He coughs)

ANTIP
I knew but I had the right—

MYSHKIN
Did you make that up yourself?

VLADIMIR
We refuse to recognize any right to ask those questions.

MYSHKIN
I only wondered if Mr. Burdovsky could bring himself—but since you seek publicity, why to you object to the presence of my friends?

LEBEDYEV
It is only through the goodness of your heart that you receive them.

EPANCHIN
Perfectly right.

MYSHKIN
Enough, Lebedyev, enough.

VLADIMIR
No, excuse me, Prince, that's not enough. Do you think we come here to quibble legality? We know we have no legal claim on you. We appeal to you on moral grounds. We don't beg, we demand. We come here with our heads erect.

ANTIP
We demand, we demand, we demand, we don't beg.

(He breaks off in a fit of coughing)

MYSHKIN
I am sorry, gentlemen. I thought it might be better for us to be perfectly open with one another. Frankly, the case struck me as a swindle—no personal reflection gentlemen. I knew none of you. If you only knew how many times I've been taken in since I came into my fortune.

VLADIMIR
Prince, you are wonderfully naïve.

MYSHKIN
At any rate, I was convinced Tchebarov was a shyster of some sort. Later, I decided Pavlishtchev might really have a son. But I was amazed he should be so willing to disgrace his mother's name. For even at that time Tchebarov threatened me with publicity.

ANTIP
The son—you've no right—you've no right.

IPPOLIT
The son is not responsible for the conduct of his father and the mother is not to blame.

(He coughs silently)

MYSHKIN
All the more reason for sparing her.

VLADIMIR
You go beyond naïveté, Prince.

IPPOLIT
But what right had you!

MYSHKIN
None. But I was amazed at Mr. Burdovsky's willingness to betray his mother's secret. I was convinced Tchebarov was a scoundrel who had egged Mr. Burdovsky on to such fraud by deceit.

VLADIMIR
This is intolerable.

MYSHKIN
It seems I agree with you in large part but for something you've left out. But what made you publish that article? If you come here with dignity why do you behave in a manner so mean?

ANTIP
Sir, sir, this, this—

IPPOLIT
As for the article, I don't approve of it. It was written by him here

(indicates Vladimir) but publicity is the legal right of all. As to the presence of your friends, we wanted them here. We only protested to preserve our rights.

VLADIMIR
That's true, we agreed about that.

MYSHKIN
But why did you begin by making such a fuss, then?

VLADIMIR
As to the article, it is severe, I grant. But how can one let such a flagrant case pass? As to the guilty, so much the worse. The public benefit before everything. The beneficial example. As to the facts, I had them on very good authority.

MYSHKIN
But why did you publish the article without being sure I did not intend to satisfy your claim? I tell you plainly before everyone here that I will.

AGLAIA
This is insufferable.

MADAME EPANCHIN
Heavens!

MYSHKIN
Allow me, please. When this attorney, Mr. Tchebarov, made his appearance I was convinced he had taken advantage of your simplicity, Mr. Burdovsky—

ANTIP
You've no right. I am not simple—it's—

IPPOLIT
This is insulting to the highest degree.

MYSHKIN
I decided that Mr. Burdovsky must be a simple person and that therefore I must help him. First by opposing Mr.

Tchebarov and then by giving him ten thousand rubles.

IPPOLIT
What? Only ten thousand?

ANTIP
I won't agree to take ten thousand.

VLADIMIR
Antip, take it, take it. Afterwards, we shall see.

IPPOLIT
We are not fools, Mr. Myshkin, whatever your grand friends may think.

MYSHKIN
In the first place, my fortune is not as large as you take it to be. In the second place Pavlishtchev never spent anywhere near ten thousand rubles on me. I cannot offer him more than what is due him. But why are you getting angry, gentlemen? Ah, it's as I thought. Mr. Burdovsky is a helpless man like me. That's why I entrusted Ganya Ivolgin with this matter. He told me this morning that he had proof the whole thing was a swindle and that Mr. Burdovsky was not the son of Pavlishtchev at all. I am sure it was all got up by Mr. Tchebarov. I shall, of course, be glad to give up ten thousand in memory of Mr. Pavlishtchev but it must go to a school. Ganya, please explain to them as you did to me.

GANYA
(Bows ironically) You do not deny, Mr. Burdovsky, you were born two years after your mother was legally married? The date can be too easily proved.

IPPOLIT
No, no. There was a mistake in the article.

GANYA

Well, then it may be easily shown that you are not his son, for Mr. Pavlishtchev was in Germany for a whole year previous to your birth. I have obtained a letter so proving. If you wish to see proof and experts to examine the handwriting—

BURDOVSKY

If it is so, I've been deceived, deceived not by Tchebarov but long before. I don't want any experts. I don't want to see you. I believe you. I withdraw my claim. I want no money. Goodbye.

GANYA

If you could stay a few moments Mr. Burdovsky, I may have turned up a few facts of which you would not care to remain in ignorance.

VLADIMIR

Antip, I told you before, it was not certain.

GANYA

Mr. Burdovsky could hardly have known that Pavlishtchev was absent from Russian twenty years ago.

IPPOLIT

Allow me, what's all this rigmarole for? We accept the fact the case is over. Are you trying to show what a clever detective you are?

GANYA

Don't get so excited. I only wish to reassure Mr. Burdovsky that Mr. Pavlishtchev's relations with his mother were honorable whatever appearances there may have been to the contrary. Those appearances gave rise to gossip. You see Mr. Burdovsky, Pavlishtchev was in love with your mother's sister but the marriage was prevented. Before you were born the lady died. Your mother was about ten at the time and she was an orphan. Mr. Pavlishtchev brought her up as his own daughter. He provided her with a dowry. After she was married he continued to allow her money. It was after your birth that her husband moved to another town. It was there that the situation was misunderstood and the rumors started. Then Mr. Pavlishtchev died suddenly without leaving a will.

VLADIMIR
This is disgusting.

IPPOLIT
It really is insupportable. What's the object of it?

GANYA
I simply wish Mr. Burdovsky to know I look upon him as an honorable man. Everyone, even Tchebarov, was behaving honorably. Mr. Burdovsky took up his defense not in his own interest but in the service of truth and progress, that is why we offer you—

MYSHKIN
Ganya, don't insult them—

ANTIP
I don't want your money. Here is the money you sent me! How dared you! How dared you!

IPPOLIT
Two hundred and fifty rubles as charity!

(He coughs)

AGLAIA
The article said a hundred.

MYSHKIN
I am to blame. I ventured to offer you ten thousand, I

ought to have done it differently but now I can't because you despise me.

MADAME EPANCHIN
This is a madhouse.

AGLAIA
How can you humble yourself before them? They are not fit to shine your shoes. How can you humble me like this? Mother, do something!

VLADIMIR
Yes, Prince, one must do you justice. You know how to offer your friendship and your money in a way that it's impossible for an honorable man to take it under any circumstances. You're either a bit too innocent or a bit too clever. You know best which.

GANYA
Excuse me, but there's only a hundred rubles here.

MYSHKIN
Let it be, let it be, Ganya.

VLADIMIR
No, don't let it be. That's a hundred and fifty rubles missing. That's not merely a detail. The point is we refuse your charity. We'll pay back your hundred and fifty rubles.

MADAME EPANCHIN
I shall lose my mind here. Enough. It's time to call a halt to this nonsense. Enough, Ivan Fyodorovitch! Let me alone. You hadn't the sense to take me away before. You are the head of the family. You might have thought of your wife and daughter. Now we can find the way out of this chaos and infamy without you.

(To Myshkin) So you ask their forgiveness for offering

them a fortune?

(To Vladimir) And what are you laughing about you brag-
gart? You know the Prince will offer it again tomorrow.

(To Myshkin) You will, won't you? Won't you?

MYSHKIN
I shall.

AGLAIA
You can't. You can't degrade yourself like this. I won't let
you.

MADAME EPANCHIN
So, that's what you're reckoning on. I see through you all.

VLADIMIR
There's chaos and infamy to be found everywhere, Madame.

MADAME EPANCHIN
But not so bad. Not so bad as yours. This stuttering fellow
won't take your money. But I'll bet he'd murder you.
That's not dishonorable. That's just noble indignation.
They come here with their noses in the air and behave like
lackeys. And then you go and beg their pardons. Isn't it
chaos? Isn't it infamy? So you'll go to them tomorrow,
Prince?

MYSHKIN
Yes.

MADAME EPANCHIN
Then I don't want to know you. And you'll go to this atheist, too?

(Indicating Ippolit) How dare you laugh at me?

AGLAIA
Maman, this is shameful.

IPPOLIT
Don't worry, young lady, she cannot attack a dying man. I shall be very glad to explain why I laughed.

(He coughs blood)

MADAME EPANCHIN
He is dying, yet he must hold forth. You are not fit for talking. You should simply go lie down.

IPPOLIT
I shall. I shall as soon as I go home. I shall be dead in a fortnight. I should like to say two words to you at parting.

MADAME EPANCHIN
Are you crazy? You want nursing. It's not time to talk. Go to bed.

IPPOLIT
If I go to bed, I shan't get up again till I die. I would have done so yesterday, but I put it off so I could come here. Only I am awfully tired—

MADAME EPANCHIN
Sit down. Sit down. Here's a chair.

IPPOLIT
Thank you, thank you and you sit down so we can talk. This is the last time I shall be out in the air. I am not very sentimental, but I am awfully glad all this happened here.

MADAME EPANCHIN
You can't talk. You can hardly breathe.

IPPOLIT
I shall be better in a minute. Why do you want to refuse my last wish? I know you are good natured—the Prince is good natured—we are all ridiculously good natured.

MADAME EPANCHIN
(Sits) That's true. Only don't get excited. You've softened my heart. But I am not going to apologize to anyone.

IPPOLIT
You seem to think we were shameless in our article. But we got our information from none other than that gentleman over there.

(He indicates Lebedyev)

MADAME EPANCHIN
Is it true?

LEBEDYEV
It's holy truth.

MADAME EPANCHIN
Why, he seems proud of it!

LEBEDYEV
I'm abject, abject. I feel it.

MADAME EPANCHIN
How can you have anything to do with such a creature, Prince? I will never forgive you.

LEBEDYEV
The Prince will forgive me.

IPPOLIT
(Laughs) I know the Prince will forgive him. I've learned to respect the Prince extremely. You know it's all very

funny. Burdovsky wanted to vindicate his mother. The Prince sincerely wants to help Burdovsky. And here they stand like enemies. You all hate Burdovsky because you think his conduct has been unseemly, rude, no matter how sincere. Appearances, that's all you care for. I'm sure that no one has loved his mother as Burdovsky has. I know, Prince, you've sent Burdovsky's mother money on the sly. Now Burdovsky will accuse you of indelicacy. I swear that's how it will be. Ha, Ha, Ha.

(He chokes)

MADAME EPANCHIN
Are you through? Now go to bed.

IPPOLIT
I shall say goodbye. General, I have the honor of inviting you to my funeral. All of you—in the wake of the General.

MADAME EPANCHIN
You had better rest the night here.

IPPOLIT
Do you know I came here to see the trees? That's not ridiculous, is it? Do you know I am not eighteen? Do you know why you are afraid of us? You are afraid of our sincerity—though you despise me.

MADAME EPANCHIN
No one despises you, sit down.

IPPOLIT
Ah, it's a good thing that I am dying. I am too sincere, too sensitive. If it weren't for this consumption I should have killed myself. What does my sincerity, my sensitivity mean to anyone? It convinces no one. It makes them laugh. Please don't laugh at the foolish fellow—

MADAME EPANCHIN
Do tell me, Ivan Fyodorovitch, what is to be done now?
Be so good as to break your majestic silence—

MYSHKIN
I shall be very glad if he will stay here.

IPPOLIT
No. I am going with them.

(Indicating by his attempt to join them Vladimir and Antip)

MYSHKIN
Ah, that is what I was afraid of.

IPPOLIT
Ah, you were afraid of that were you? I hate every one of
you. I hate you all, every one of you, but you most, you
idiotic, philanthropic, millionaire. This has all been your
contriving—you planned this. You led me on to breaking
down. You drove a dying man to shame. I don't want your
help. Don't you dare triumph!

LEBEDYEV
He is ashamed of his tears. That was bound to happen.
Bravo, Prince, you saw right through him.

MYSHKIN
I invite you to stay here among the trees as long as you
like.

IPPOLIT
Well that does it! What right have you? What right? That's
the last straw. Well, I won't stay. But I want to tell you a
little story before I go. I had intended to write it but why
bother? It is for your benefit, yours all of you—it is dedi-
cated to you—so why bother to write it when I can tell it
just as easily?

EPANCHIN
Hadn't you better not?

VLADIMIR
Ippolit?

GANYA
Don't really—

IPPOLIT
So I'm not to tell it? Are you afraid?

MYSHKIN
What of?

IPPOLIT
If you don't want to hear it, you don't have to stay. I don't force anyone—

MADAME EPANCHIN
He orders people out of another person's house. Wonderful.

GANYA
And how if we all get up and go away?

IPPOLIT
You don't like me, at all.

MYSHKIN
Couldn't you tell us later?

IPPOLIT
I want to tell it now. It is the story of an eighteen-year-old boy who is dying of consumption. He comes with his friend to help that friend to vindicate a wrong that was done his mother. It turns out there was nothing to vindicate. It was all an embarrassing mistake. But the person to

whom they have applied is not satisfied. He must humiliate them with his charity. He invites this boy to stay at his villa so that he can cough out his remaining days under the smug eyes of his benefactor. He wishes to put the consumptive under obligations. He knows the boy loves sunshine. How can he refuse? He will die there feeling grateful to his benefactor having thus expiated the wrong of having been rude to that great person. He will see how magnanimous is this noble Prince. And end his life in abject humiliation. If he refuses, why he behaves like a churl. What right has this Prince to put him in such a position? There is no alternative left for the young man but suicide. As it happens he has a pistol in his pocket. He ends his life right there before the Prince and all his friends after having given his explanation.

MADAME EPANCHIN
Good heavens, he will kill himself.

(She goes and throws her arms around him)

GANYA
He will not kill himself.

EPANCHIN
No, he will not shoot himself. This is all braggadocio.

GANYA
It's absolutely nothing to me.

LEBEDYEV
You can't let him do that here.

ANTIP
He has the right. He has the right.

IPPOLIT
You are really very eager to see me do it. Did you imagine

that I did not foresee all this hatred? I shall go. Let me go.

MYSHKIN
Let him go.

VLADIMIR
Yes, let him go.

IPPOLIT
(Pulls out his pistol and attempts to shoot himself)

(There is a click but no report)

MADAME EPANCHIN
Good heavens!

GANYA
It did not fire.

(The gun is taken from Ippolit by Ganya)

EPANCHIN
It was not loaded. Sheer braggadocio—

GANYA
It was loaded. The cap is missing.

ANTIP
If-anyone-ever-insinuates-that-he-knew-the-pistol-was-
not-in-proper-order-he-will-have-to-answer-to-me!

(Ippolit has completely broken down)

MYSHKIN
Put him to bed, Ganya. He will not harm himself again.

(Ganya and Lebedyev lead off the sobbing Ippolit)

MADAME EPANCHIN

We must thank you, Prince, for the agreeable entertainment you have given us all. Come along home, Aglaia.

ANTIP

And we shall go, too, Prince.

(The Prince remains alone and finally sinks down in a garden seat)

(Nastasya Fillipovna enters. She is watchful as if she might have been followed. She has obviously been hiding for some time.)

NASTASYA

Are you happy? Only say one word to me. Are you happy now? Today, this minute? She was here. What did she say?

MYSHKIN

Calm yourself, calm yourself.

NASTASYA

I love you, Myshkin. Don't be angry. I don't put myself on a level with you. I want you to be happy. Happy with her.

MYSHKIN

But she does not love me. In fact, she told me so just now although why I can't say. I had never spoken of it to her.

NASTASYA

Are you in love with her?

MYSHKIN

I have been, yes, without knowing it.

NASTASYA

That must be why she told you she wasn't in love with

you. To put the idea in your head.

MYSHKIN
I have heard that you are trying to bring us together.
Really, Nastasya....

NASTASYA
I am doing it for my own sake. In renouncing you I re-
nounce the world. I am dead now. Do you know how I
know? I see it in Rogozhin's eyes. Those eyes are silent
but I know their secret. I always fancied he had a corpse
hidden in the house...that house of his...so dark. A corpse
wrapped in leather under the floorboards.

MYSHKIN
You should marry him or set him free.

NASTASYA
I can't. You are innocent. And in your innocence lies all
your perfection. What have you to do with my passion for
you? Nothing. My love is my own. You are now alto-
gether mine. I shall be all my life beside you. Goodbye,
my darling.

(Pause) I shall soon die.

(She runs out)

(Aglaia returns)

AGLAIA
Was that Nastasya Fillipovna?

MYSHKIN
Yes.

AGLAIA
(Unexpectedly) Why did that young man try to kill him-

self?

MYSHKIN
Because he wanted us to tell him that we loved him very much and that we respected him.

AGLAIA
I uscd to do that when I was a little girl. I thought I'd poison myself. I would lie in my coffin and they would weep over me. You have no right to be so harsh with him. You have no tenderness, nothing but truth so you judge harshly.

MYSHKIN
Why did you come back?

AGLAIA
I told Maman that I forgot my gloves. But that was a fa-la-la.

MYSHKIN
A fa-la-la?

AGLAIA
A lie, silly. I came back because I want to make you a proposition that you should be my friend. Why are you staring at me all of a sudden? Perhaps, you don't care to accept my proposition—?

MYSHKIN
But I don't really understand.

AGLAIA
Why do you suppose I came back? Perhaps you look on me as a fool as they do at home?

MYSHKIN
I didn't know they looked on you as a fool. I don't look on you so.

AGLAIA
You don't look on me so? Very clever on your part. Particularly cleverly expressed.

MYSHKIN
I think you are very clever. When you said there's no tenderness, only truth in me and it is unjust, perhaps you hit on something. I shall remember that and think it over.

AGLAIA
I've wanted to tell you this for a long time. You're better than any of them. You're mentally afflicted but the mind that matters in you is better than in any of them. It's something, in fact, they have never dreamed of. I told the others that. I think only Maman understood.

MYSHKIN
You are like your Maman.

AGLAIA
Thank you. You have a great respect for her then?

MYSHKIN
Yes.

AGLAIA
I'm glad because people sometimes laugh at her. I've been thinking a long time and at last I've picked you out. I don't want them to laugh at me anymore. I don't want to have suitors. I want—I want—well I want to run away from home and I want you to help me.

MYSHKIN
I don't believe it.

AGLAIA
Yes, yes, yes! Run away from home. I don't want to be teased about marriage anymore. I want to tell someone

everything and so I've chosen you. I want to speak freely of everything. They suddenly began saying that I was waiting for you and that I loved you. I don't want to get married. I don't want to be a useless social butterfly. I propose to take up teaching. Couldn't we go in for education together?

MYSHKIN
I want to help, Aglaia, but are you serious?

AGLAIA
If you won't consent I shall marry...Ganya. I don't want to be looked at as a horrid girl and accused of goodness knows what.

MYSHKIN
Are you mad? Who accuses you? And of what?

AGLAIA
Everyone. For two years now. I read a French novel because I wanted to find out what was what. Do you know papa tried to convince me I didn't understand what was meant? I told them I'm not a little girl. Maman almost fainted when she heard me.

MYSHKIN
Of course, you're not. Have you always lived at home?

AGLAIA
I've never been anywhere. Why are you laughing at me? Don't make me angry. You must think I'm in love with you and that I'm making a tryst with you.

MYSHKIN
I confess that I was afraid earlier that you might be; now I see—

AGLAIA

You dared to imagine! Do you think I've come all the way back alone so that we shall be caught and compromised and that you might be forced to marry me?

MYSHKIN

You should be ashamed. How could you let such a nasty idea enter your innocent heart?

AGLAIA

I'm not ashamed at all. How do you know that my heart is so innocent? I'm sorry. I used a very stupid expression. I said that just—to test you. Take it as though it were un-said.

(Pause, then forcing herself)

MYSHKIN

—what was that woman doing here?

MYSHKIN

Oh, if I could tell you everything.

AGLAIA

I know everything! You lived for a whole month in the same flat with that woman with whom you ran away.

(Pause) I don't love you at all.

(Pause) I love Ganya.

MYSHKIN

That is not true.

AGLAIA

Then am I lying? I gave my word day before yesterday in this very garden.

MYSHKIN
That's not true. You've invented all that.

AGLAIA
You're wonderfully polite. Let me tell you he's reformed. He loves me more than his life. He burned his hand before my eyes to prove it.

MYSHKIN
Burned his hand?

AGLAIA
Yes, his left hand. You may believe it or not, I don't care.

MYSHKIN
Did he bring a candle with him?

AGLAIA
Yes. What's so unusual about that?

MYSHKIN
A whole one? A candlestick?

AGLAIA
Oh, well no. A half one—a candle end. It doesn't matter. Let me alone. He left his finger in it a whole half an hour.

MYSHKIN
His hands weren't burned yesterday.

AGLAIA
Do you know why I told you that fib just now? When you lie you must be able to add a little something eccentric to give it the ring of truth. It didn't work because I didn't do it properly. I wanted to put you to shame for your behavior.

MYSHKIN
My behavior?

AGLAIA
Yes, yours and hers.

MYSHKIN
You are unjust to me.

AGLAIA
What was she doing here? Six months ago you offered her your hand in the presence of everyone. Don't interrupt me. Then she ran off with Rogozhin. Then she ran from him to you and back to him again. And here you are on her trail again. It was for her sake, for her sake you came here, wasn't it?

MYSHKIN
Yes, for her sake. To help her.

AGLAIA
How I despise you.

MYSHKIN
There isn't really much I can to do help her.

AGLAIA
If you came not knowing why then you love her very much.

MYSHKIN
No, I don't love her. If only you knew with what horror I recall the time I spent with her.

AGLAIA
Tell me everything.

MYSHKIN

I've wanted to. That poor girl thinks she is the most fallen, the most vicious creature in the whole world. She says otherwise but she believes it. She believes it. She ran from me because she wanted to do something shameful. Then she could punish herself for doing it.

AGLAIA

Did you ever preach such sermons to her?

MYSHKIN

Oh, no. I loved her too much to talk. But afterwards she guessed all.

AGLAIA

What did she guess?

MYSHKIN

That I only pitied her, that I didn't love her anymore.

AGLAIA

How do you know she doesn't love Rogozhin?

MYSHKIN

She only laughs at him.

AGLAIA

And did she ever laugh at you?

MYSHKIN

No.

AGLAIA

Do you know she writes me letters?

MYSHKIN

I have heard so. I didn't believe it.

AGLAIA

Do you know what she writes me?

MYSHKIN

I can imagine. I shouldn't be surprised at anything.

AGLAIA

She wants me to marry you. She tells me that you love me. Did you tell her you were in love with me?

MYSHKIN

Not until today.

AGLAIA

You mean you are?

MYSHKIN

Yes.

AGLAIA

(Not pursuing it) What am I to do with this situation? I cannot go on receiving them.

MYSHKIN

I'll try to make her stop.

AGLAIA

Then you're a man of no heart! Surely you must see she loves only you. These letters, do you know what they mean? It's jealousy. Do you suppose she really will marry Rogozhin? She'll kill herself on her wedding day.

MYSHKIN

God knows, Aglaia, I would give up my life to help her. But I can't love her now, and she knows it.

AGLAIA

Then sacrifice yourself: it's just in your line. And don't

call me Aglaia. You ought to raise her up. Why, you do love her, you know.

MYSHKIN
I can't sacrifice myself like that, not anymore. In her pride she will never forgive me for my love and we shall both come to ruin. Just as she will with Rogozhin. Can there be love after what I've gone through? No, it's something else, not love.

AGLAIA
But you've come here for her sake, not to marry me?

MYSHKIN
Yes, for her sake.

AGLAIA
(Angry) You may say, you may believe that your woman is insane, but I have nothing to do with such insane fantasies. I beg you, Prince, take these letters and fling them back to her from me. And if she dares write to me again tell her I shall complain to my father and have her put into a house of correction.

MYSHKIN
You can't feel like that. It's not true.

AGLAIA
It's the truth! It's the truth!

MADAME EPANCHIN
(Entering) What's the truth? What's the truth?

AGLAIA
It's the truth that I am going to marry Ganya! That I love Ganya and that I'm going to run away from home with him tomorrow. Do you hear? Is that enough for you?

(She runs away)

MADAME EPANCHIN
You'll be so kind as to give an explanation.

(At this moment a knife thuds into the tree next to which Myshkin is standing) Good lord! Those nihilists have tried to assassinate you.

MYSHKIN
No, it's Rogozhin's knife.

MADAME EPANCHIN
What will you do?

MYSHKIN
(Wearily) Give it back to him.

CURTAIN

ACT III

Scene 6

Summer—Lebedyev's garden. A small walled garden with several entrances. Many trees. Lebedyev's house is to the right of the audience.

(At rise, Lebedyev is sitting morosely, Myshkin enters)

MYSHKIN
Why so gloomy, Lebedyev?

LEBEDYEV
I have encountered a severe calamity in the last twenty-four hours.

MYSHKIN
What's the matter?

LEBEDYEV
I have lost twenty-four rubles from my coat pocket.

MYSHKIN
How did it happen?

LEBEDYEV
The fruits of drinking. I left the pocket book in the over-coat when I changed coats in the hall. It is true when God will chastise a man he first will deprive him of all reason. I got drunk and forgot about it till this morning.

MYSHKIN
Could you have dropped it?

LEBEDYEV
Anything is possible. But I never left the house. If I dropped it according to the laws of nature and of nature's God the article would be on the floor. It is not on the floor.

MYSHKIN
Perhaps, you put it somewhere?

LEBEDYEV
I've been through everything.

MYSHKIN
Perhaps, someone found it?

LEBEDYEV
Or picked my pocket. If they found it they would have come forward—they have not come forward.

MYSHKIN
This distresses me very much. But who? That's the question.

LEBEDYEV
You define the problem with wonderful exactitude, Prince.

MYSHKIN
Do you suspect anyone?

LEBEDYEV
The servant is out of the question. So are my children. One of the visitors then.

MYSHKIN
Utterly impossible.

LEBEDYEV
Utterly impossible. But so it must be! I could hardly have robbed myself.

MYSHKIN
There is Ganya, his father General Ivolgin, Ferdy-shtchenko, and Ippolit Terentyev. I exclude the General.

LEBEDYEV
Of course. You wouldn't have me suspect Ganya?

MYSHKIN
What folly!

LEBEDYEV
Or Mr. Terentyev, who is dying?

MYSHKIN
No.

LEBEDYEV
That leaves Ferdyshtchenko.

MYSHKIN
Yes, but proof is necessary.

LEBEDYEV
Yes, yes. I told the General of my plight. He was indignant beyond anything I expected. He has agreed to help me find either the purse or the thief. In fact, the General suspects Mr. Ferdyshtchenko. He told me so.

MYSHKIN
Yes. I heard of it from Ganya before he left.

LEBEDYEV
When did he leave?

MYSHKIN
Around six-fifteen. His usual time.

LEBEDYEV
That's interesting. He must have gotten up before six to tell Ganya of his suspicions of Ferdyshtchenko. Whereas I did not learn of the robbery until after seven.

MYSHKIN
Listen, Lebedyev. Keep quite about it, I beg you.

LEBEDYEV
I'm abject, Prince. But I don't like to cause pain. Don't worry about it.

(Rogozhin enters the garden)

ROGOZHIN
(To Lebedyev) Vanish, scum.

LEBEDYEV
Monster!

(He runs off)

ROGOZHIN
I haven't been long finding you.

MYSHKIN
Why have you come?

ROGOZHIN
I hear you're going to marry Aglaia Ivanova.

MYSHKIN
Yes, it's all agreed.

ROGOZHIN
You know I am to be married the same day?

MYSHKIN
Yes, yes.

ROGOZHIN
You're a strange fellow.

MYSHKIN
Why are you so bitter against me? Because you tried to kill me? I tell you I only remember that we exchanged crosses. I look upon what happened as madness. I understand how you felt. Let there be no anger between us.

ROGOZHIN
As though you could feel anger.

MYSHKIN
You still hate me so.

ROGOZHIN
I don't like you. You are kind. You have never deceived me. You never will. But I don't like you, all the same. What makes you think I've repented of it?

MYSHKIN
Perhaps you can't. I don't ask you to. As long as you think she loves me and not you, you can't help it. But, perhaps, she only uses that as a pretext to torment you, because she loves you more than anyone.

ROGOZHIN
I'm afraid not. But I understand you've been having the same sort of treatment.

MYSHKIN
What have you heard?

ROGOZHIN
I see now it's true. I didn't come here without a purpose. Aglaia Ivanova wants to meet Nastasya here, now in our presence. They should be along shortly.

MYSHKIN
Is it possible?

ROGOZHIN
I was detailed to get you.

MYSHKIN
But why? At whose suggestion? For what reason?

ROGOZHIN
At your fiancée's suggestion for reasons we'll soon learn. Here they come. Don't they look sweet? Oh, are they jealous.

MYSHKIN
Aglaia, what's this all about?

AGLAIA
You'll see. Nastasya Fillipovna and I have become great friends, haven't we, dear?

NASTASYA
It was very charming.

AGLAIA
You know, of course, why I asked you to come?

NASTASYA
No, I haven't the slightest idea.

AGLAIA
You understand everything, but you pretend you don't on purpose.

NASTASYA
Why should I?

AGLAIA
You want to take advantage of my position. I am, as it were, your hostess since I invited you.

NASTASYA
You're responsible for that, not I. I don't know what your object is.

AGLAIA
Restrain your tongue. That is your weapon. I've not come to fight you with it.

NASTASYA
Ah, you have come to fight then! Would you believe it, I thought you were more intelligent.

AGLAIA
You misunderstand me. I don't like you but I have not come here to fight you.

NASTASYA
Why have you come then?

AGLAIA
I came to speak to you as one human being to another.

NASTASYA
And how do two human beings speak to one another?

AGLAIA
You have written me letters. I want to answer them in person. In your letters you ask me to marry the Prince.

NASTASYA
Yes. And you have agreed.

AGLAIA

But not because of you. I felt sorry for the Prince because he is a simple hearted man. I know the story of his unhappy love for you. You were incapable of loving him. You could not love him for you love nothing but your own shame and the delicious thought that you have been injured and wronged.

MYSHKIN

Aglaia, stop it. Aglaia, I knew you would come back here. I knew he would follow you. I felt dreadfully hurt and wounded on his account. Don't laugh. If you laugh you are not worthy to understand that.

NASTASYA

You see that I am not laughing.

AGLAIA

It's nothing to me, laugh as much as you like. When I began to question him he told me that he no longer loved you but the memory of it pierced his heart. I knew from the way he talked that anyone who chose could deceive him and still find forgiveness. That is why I came to him.

NASTASYA

I loved him, and for the same reason!

AGLAIA

(Cutting) No doubt you understand now what I want of you.

NASTASYA

Perhaps, but tell me yourself.

AGLAIA

I want to learn from you what right you have to meddle with his feelings for me? What right have you to declare to either of us that you love him after running away from him in such an insulting and degrading way?

NASTASYA
I have never told you or him that I love him. But you are right: I did run away from him.

AGLAIA
What about those letters? Who asked you to begin match-making? I thought at first you wanted to turn me against him by reminding me of his connection with you.

NASTASYA
No! I never meant that.

AGLAIA
No. I came to see that. You thought you were being noble. You're playing the role. Why don't you marry Rogozhin, who loves you and would make you happy if you'd only let him, instead of you pretending to be a martyr? He says your head is turned by poetry because you live in idleness.

NASTASYA
And you don't live in idleness?

AGLAIA
How dare you speak to me like that?

NASTASYA
(Surprised) I don't see that I have been rude to you.

AGLAIA
If you want to be a respectable woman why didn't you give up your seducer, Totsky, without all the histrionics?

NASTASYA
What do you know of the situation that you assume the right to judge me?

AGLAIA

I know you didn't go off to work. Oh, no. You went to Rogozhin so you can go on posing as a fallen angel. I don't wonder that Totsky thought it worth seventy-five thousand rubles to get rid of you. God, the wages of sin.

NASTASYA

Stop it! Stop it! You don't understand at all.

MYSHKIN

Aglaia, you're being unjust.

AGLAIA

If you wanted to be respectable you'd have become a washerwoman.

NASTASYA

Look at her! Look at her! And I thought you were an angel. Since you won't tell why you have come here I'll tell you. You've come because you're afraid.

AGLAIA

(Amazed) Afraid of you?

NASTASYA

Yes, because you still don't know which of us he loves best. And you're fearfully jealous.

AGLAIA

(Faltering) He told me that he hates you.

NASTASYA

Perhaps; I am not worthy of him. Only, only, I think you're lying! He cannot hate me, cannot hate me, Aglaia; he could not have said so.

AGLAIA

(Childishly) He does. He does! Tell her so, Myshkin, tell

her so, or I shall hate you forever.

NASTASYA
I'm not afraid of you. I've only to tell him and he'll throw you up forever and marry me at once. Do you hear? At once!

AGLAIA
(Terrified) No!

NASTASYA
And you'll have to run home alone. Shall I? Shall I?

AGLAIA
If you don't come with me at once, if you don't take me, if you don't give her up, she can have you. I don't want you.

NASTASYA
Myshkin, will you turn away from me?

MYSHKIN
(Appealing to Aglaia) Don't do this to me!

AGLAIA
You hesitate. You hesitate. I don't want you. I hate you.

(She runs) To her...go to her, you loose woman! I don't care. I'll marry Ganya. Go to her.

(Myshkin runs toward her, but it is too late)

MYSHKIN
Aglaia!

NASTASYA
You follow her? Her?

(She faints, but Myshkin has returned and folded her in his

arms) Mine, mine! Is that proud young lady gone? Why should I give you up to her? Go away, Rogozhin.

(Rogozhin looks at them and picks up his hat. He is beaten and he knows it.) Will you marry me, Prince?

MYSHKIN
If you wish it, Nastasya.

(Rogozhin walks out without looking back)

NASTASYA
My God, my God, what am I doing to you?

CURTAIN

ACT III

Scene 7

The same garden. A morning in the fall. The trees are bare and there are leaves on the ground.

Lebedyev enters the garden. The Prince is alone, dejected. It is brisk autumn.

MYSHKIN
Have you heard any news of Nastasya?

LEBEDYEV
None, Prince.

MYSHKIN
Why did she go back to Rogozhin on our wedding day? Why?

LEBEDYEV
I do not know, Prince.

MYSHKIN
I went to his house this morning and stood there for an hour. No one answered, but I'd swear someone was watching me from behind the curtain.

LEBEDYEV
You can't follow her forever.

MYSHKIN
No, no. But I must know that she is safe.

LEBEDYEV
If there's news I'll tell you. Perhaps if we changed the subject.

MYSHKIN
Yes, yes, change the subject. Have you found the four hundred rubles?

LEBEDYEV
Why yes, in fact, I have.

MYSHKIN
Thank God.

LEBEDYEV
It is no small matter to a man in my humble circumstances.

MYSHKIN
But how did you find it?

LEBEDYEV
Very simple, I found it under the chair on which my coat had been hung.

MYSHKIN
But that's impossible. Why, you told me yourself you had searched everywhere. Suddenly it turns up.

LEBEDYEV
Suddenly it turns up.

MYSHKIN
And then the General?

LEBEDYEV
Ah yes, the General. I left it under the chair.

MYSHKIN
But what for?

LEBEDYEV
Oh, nothing but curiosity. I wanted the General to find it. For since I had found it, why shouldn't the General? I put it so that it was completely in view. But the General simply hasn't noticed it.

MYSHKIN
Then it is still under the chair.

LEBEDYEV
Oh, no. It vanished from under the chair and now it has turned up in the pocket of my coat. But I take no notice of it.

MYSHKIN
And the General?

LEBEDYEV
He's been angry all day. Tomorrow, though, I mean to find the pocket book.

MYSHKIN
How can you humiliate a man like that—a most honest man?

LEBEDYEV
You're right. He is honest. He lies and he steals but he's honest. I shall find it immediately.

MYSHKIN
You're an impossible fellow, Lebedyev.

LEBEDYEV
I know it. I feel it.

MYSHKIN
Where is Ganya? He usually comes at this time.

LEBEDYEV
(Uneasy) He's gone—for the day.

MYSHKIN
Oh, that's too bad. I wanted him to take a message to the Epanchins.

LEBEDYEV
Perhaps I—

MYSHKIN
I shouldn't ask you, but they refuse to admit me.

LEBEDYEV
But after all—

MYSHKIN
But I want to see Aglaia.

LEBEDYEV
But then how could you have let it happen? Aglaia will not share you with anyone.

MYSHKIN
Yes, yes, you are right. I am to blame. I never saw such hatred in anyone's eyes.

LEBEDYEV
But she is a mad woman.

MYSHKIN
No, I am speaking of Aglaia. She was terrible.

LEBEDYEV
Yes, and there was no reason for her to feel that way. It was only your pity for Nastasya Fillipovna. It was your inexperience. From the very first it began with falsity, that night I met you for the first time and you offered her your hand. It was a democratic feeling on your part; a sense of chivalry not love that motivated you. And you were exhausted by travel, your head was spinning.

MYSHKIN
Yes, yes, that's exactly how it was—

LEBEDYEV
You were intoxicated with enthusiasm. The question is whether it was genuine emotion or intellectual enthusiasm! After all, she may not have deserved scorn, but did she deserve praise?

MYSHKIN
Yes, that all may be so.

LEBEDYEV
Could all her suffering justify such pride?

MYSHKIN
But compassion?

LEBEDYEV
Yes, but how could you humiliate Aglaia out of compassion for Nastasya? Was Aglaia suffering less than Nastasya? How could you allow it?

MYSHKIN
I didn't allow it. I was running after Aglaia when Nastasya fell down fainting. And since then they haven't let me see Aglaia.

LEBEDYEV
But you still should have run after Aglaia.

MYSHKIN
But Nastasya would have killed herself. Oh, if Aglaia would only let me explain. She will understand. She will understand.

LEBEDYEV
After you were going to marry Nastasya again?

MYSHKIN
But I was just marrying her, that's all. She wanted me to. I had to until she ran away.

LEBEDYEV
You were going to marry her without loving her then?

MYSHKIN
No, no. I love her with my whole heart. Why she's a child. Quite a child.

LEBEDYEV
And you love Aglaia too?

MYSHKIN
Yes. Yes.

LEBEDYEV
Then you want to love both of them? Think what you're saying.

MYSHKIN
Without Aglaia I'm—I must see her. If only I could tell her everything. There's something in all this that I can't explain to you, I can't find the words. Aglaia will understand.

LEBEDYEV
No, Prince, she won't understand. She loved you like a woman not like an abstract spirit. Do you know, my poor Prince, the most likely thing is that you've never loved either of them.

MYSHKIN
I don't know. Perhaps, you're very clever, Lebedyev, but I don't know. For God's sake let's go to her. For God's sake!

LEBEDYEV
She's not here, Prince.

MYSHKIN
Listen, I'll write to her. You take a letter.

LEBEDYEV
Spare me such a commission, Prince. I've been trying to tell you—she eloped with Ganya this morning.

MYSHKIN
Have I lost her then?

LEBEDYEV
(Going) I am sorry, Prince—

(Lebedyev goes out, Rogozhin enters from the garden)

ROGOZHIN
Come with me, brother, I want you.

MYSHKIN
Where is she?

ROGOZHIN
At my house.

MYSHKIN
How is she feeling? Is she upset?

ROGOZHIN
No, she is not upset.

MYSHKIN
Was it you who looked at me from behind the curtain?

ROGOZHIN
Yes.

MYSHKIN
The porter said no one was home.

ROGOZHIN
The porter doesn't know. We were both there; she and I. But we were being very quiet.

MYSHKIN
It's dark in your house.

ROGOZHIN
We'll need candles.

MYSHKIN
Is she dead?

ROGOZHIN
Yes.

MYSHKIN
You—was it—you?

ROGOZHIN
It was I.

MYSHKIN
I had a foreboding.

ROGOZHIN
I came so that we could spend this night together. All three of us. We'll put her between us.

MYSHKIN
Yes, yes—

ROGOZHIN
We won't let them take her away.

MYSHKIN
Not on any account. Certainly not.

ROGOZHIN
That's what I've decided. Not to give her up on any account to anyone. We must be very quiet.

MYSHKIN
Oh, we'll be quiet. Very quiet.

ROGOZHIN
I've been with her ever since. All the time. I only left her to get you. She wants you there.

MYSHKIN
Yes, yes, of course.

ROGOZHIN
The only thing I am afraid of is the smell.

MYSHKIN
Let's get flowers.

ROGOZHIN
But it will make us sad to see her with flowers all around

her.

MYSHKIN
Tell me, did you do it with the knife...the same one?

ROGOZHIN
The same one.

MYSHKIN
Tell me. At my wedding. At the church door. Did you mean to kill her then?

ROGOZHIN
I don't know.

MYSHKIN
Was there a great deal of blood?

ROGOZHIN
None at all.

MYSHKIN
Then she's still pretty?

ROGOZHIN
Come along. She's waiting for you.

MYSHKIN
Yes. Shh. We'd better hurry. We have only tonight. And I think I can hear footsteps. Yes, footsteps.

ROGOZHIN
Footsteps?

MYSHKIN
Yes, they're trying to take her away from us. We must hurry and bolt the door. We must hurry.

ROGOZHIN
Come, brother.

(Rogozhin supports the excited Myshkin off as the curtain descends)

CURTAIN

Printed in Great Britain
by Amazon

75048303R00095